PRACTISING COMMUNITY

Other titles by Robin Greenwood

Reclaiming the Church (Fount Original 1988)
Transforming Priesthood (SPCK 1994)

ROBIN GREENWOOD

Practising Community

The Task of the Local Church

First published in Great Britain 1996
Society for Promoting Christian Knowledge
Holy Trinity Church
Marylebone Road
London NW1 4DU

Biblical quotations are
from the *Revised Standard Version of the Bible* © 1971 and 1952,
and from the *Revised English Bible* © 1989 Oxford
and Cambridge University Presses.

British Library Cataloguing-in-Publication Data
A catalogue record of this book is available from
the British Library

ISBN 0-281-04916-5

Typeset by Datix International, Bungay, Suffolk
Printed in Great Britain by
Biddles Ltd, Guildford and King's Lynn

To Claire, who shares the struggle

CONTENTS

Preface ix

Introduction 1

1. Local Ministry in Practice 9

2. A Theology of the Local Church 25

3. Church Rooted in the Trinitarian God 44

4. Equal and Different Ministries 60

5. Who has Power in the Church? 81

6. Keys to Good Practice in Local
Ministry 101

Epilogue 112

Bibliography 114

Index 121

PREFACE

I should like to acknowledge the advice and help of the following in shaping my ideas and redrafting the text: Michael Allen, Lesley Bentley, Andrew Bowden, Peter Bradley, David Brindley, Stephen Brown, David Durston, Barrie Glover, Henry Grant, Hilary Ineson, Peter Kerr, Robin Mann, Geoff Mason, Caroline Pascoe, Alan Payne, David Primrose, Gabriel Robin, John M. Schofield, Malcolm Squires, and Ian Stockton.

My thanks go also to Anne MacLean and Jenny Robinson for secretarial assistance and to Lucy Gasson at SPCK for her companionship in this venture.

INTRODUCTION

This is a book about creative futures for the mission and ministry of the local church. My own experience and reflection is chiefly of the Church of England, but the issues raised here are generic to most churches today. The contemporary urgency to sustain and extend the mission of the church in each locality, together with a widening disregard for and cynicism regarding institutions, is leading to new insights about God's hopes for the Church. The sharp context of present ecumenical debate and experiment on the identity and task of the Christian community includes a clear movement towards a theology of *communion*. In the search for a more adequate understanding of Church the notion of *communion* speaks of a community of those who in unique and complementary ways are drawn into sharing in the mystery of God's gift to the world in Christ. The title *Practising Community* points to a threefold understanding of the task of the local church. First, as a doctor practises medicine, the Church practises community, following the example of Jesus. Second, the sinful and divided Church has only the capacity for practice – it is far from achieving perfection. Third, this practice is not to create an insular community but rather to demonstrate and evoke – however partially – the practice of community in all the networks of society.

This vision for the task of the Church confronts a church culture currently in danger of being dominated by anxieties about finance and steadily diminishing numbers of stipendiary clergy. The inescapable facts of the present day Church are well known. In Church of England parishes and diocesan offices shortfalls in giving are bringing about situations for which there are no instant remedies. Those with a deep concern for mission often accuse senior church leaders of planning for decline. A more mature position is to recognize that calculating how to run a diocese with fewer clergy is partly an exercise of person management and financial adeptness – but also to recognize that this is not the whole story. This book is written in the conviction that it is not sufficient to shore up the existing structures nor to maintain the inherited model of Church. Rather, I share the belief that God is summoning the Church to reframe itself by listening acutely to the new demands of mission and ministry at the opening of a new era. In a period of transition the hope that comes of commitment to prayer will be required while we live through the chaos associated with transformations of identity.

Making plans for the churches at the beginning of the third millennium will require the implementation of ideas which have evolved gradually over many years. Complex human organizations take time to make the profound changes required by altered circumstances and developing visions. Often a first step is the attempt to fend off difficulties by increasing the pace and amount of work done on the same basis as before. So the handle is cranked twice as fast, as everyone tries to solve the situation by frenetic activity. This fails. Only then comes the realization that more of the same is not solving the problems. There has to be a complete rethink of what is required.

The appropriateness of what are often called the mainline churches sustaining anything like their present appearance far into the twenty-first century is increasingly under fire. This book is not about sticking-plaster strategies nor does it advocate a retreat into congregationalism, with an affordable Church for like-minded paying customers. There is a cause to be pleaded for a fast-developing Anglicanism growing out of a dialogue between its history and the urgent demands of the present. The well-tested Anglican process of coming to truth through processes of honest and courteous debate is under threat. It will take courage, commitment, and a constantly deepening spirituality to stay with the uncertainty rather than attempt to avoid it. This book makes positive proposals for an alternative vision – at a time of insecurity and confused identity – avoiding the insidious consolation of instant clarity in the many available fundamentalisms.

Can Anglicans hold their nerve? In these ecumenical times, the Decades of Evangelism and of Solidarity with Women are encouraging an engagement with an international new theology and spirituality that rejects old party divides. A constant temptation for the Church of England has been towards an imperialist and insular approach to theology. For so much of the twentieth century the scholarship of Germany and beyond Europe has been looked on with suspicion in Britain. In fact, one of the underused assets of English Anglicanism is membership of the federation of provinces making up the Anglican Communion within the One, Holy, Catholic, and Apostolic Church. Deep engagement with key elements of the ecclesiologies of the majority part of the Anglican Communion or with those of the international ecumenical community, is usually missing in Britain. To make new plans against a universal horizon could help the Church of England to ask urgent self-critical questions, and in particular, how much of our present inheritance is of the essence of the faith and how much is the product of culture?

At a recent clergy training event, time was given to studying the essence of the Anglican quality of the Church of England. Among the attributes listed were the following: homeliness, chaplaincy to the nation, common sense, valuing the sacraments, a broad spectrum of belief and practice, openness, formed by theology and spirituality of centuries, wider than the local church, disciplined by the daily office, a prophetic voice, variety and diversity, a tapestry of music and cultures and commitment to the parochial system. There is something essentially routine about this list. Anglicans are often critical of their own commitment to transforming the ordinary. Personally I too am energized by and committed to this overall vision – but can it be transformed? Who wants such a model of Church to be reworked? Are these qualities agreed to be strengths or weaknesses? Are there enough people who really want a Church that exists for the sake of those who do not belong to it – to be prepared to pay for it? Is there sufficient courage to embrace an uncomfortably slimmed-down Church of England – in terms of professional leadership, legal niceties, and formal procedures?

In the search for new models of Church much theorizing and experimentation has been taking place in recent decades. For over fifty years Anglican writers in Britain have made their contribution to a profound international and ecumenical conversation about the possibility of a Church that is not clerically dependent. Some of the names of the chief contributors include: F. R. Barry, Roland Allen, John Robinson, A. T. Hanson, Michael Green, Michael Ramsey, Wesley Carr, John Tiller, together with official reports and discussion documents. Throughout the churches of this country personal stories, journal articles and the books of reflective practitioners have testified to a complex and slow transition in the management of local church ministry. Some of the great achievements of this movement include the fact that it is unusual today to speak of 'the' ministry, referring exclusively to clergy, or of 'going into the Church' of ordination. Instead a galaxy of ministries have been created – with enormous variety in the titles and nuances of language used to identify and describe them.

The growth in lay ministries of different kinds has been one of the 'success stories' of the Church of England over the past twenty years. There is evidence of rising expectations among lay people of active participation in the ministry of their local church.

My last book, entitled *Transforming Priesthood* (1994), showed how across the Church of England there is taking place a major transition from a traditional clerically-centred professional parochial ministry towards a way of being the local church which expects significant numbers of people to recognize and use their diverse gifts for ministry. A key element of this process is that clergy and laity *together* are becoming committed to exploring a variety of approaches to prayer and worship, education, pastoral care, evangelism, preparation for the sacraments, administration, and social responsibility.

There have been experiments for decades now in this redefining of the language and practice of ministry, even though honest appraisal suggests that in the majority of parishes some form of dependence on stipendiary clergy remains paramount. The logical next stage must be concerned with identifying, clarifying, naming and communicating the vision that – in theory at least – is gaining such wide acceptance, to enable confident steps towards good practice. Pragmatism and 'going with the flow' of local initiative should go hand-in-hand with well-tempered and transforming visions rooted in every aspect of the Christian pilgrimage. There is plenty of evidence that the traditionally conceived ways of church institutions hold little attraction for the population at large. The Spirit of God would seem to be inviting the development of a more humble, vulnerable, popular style of

Christian community that is less hierarchical and more from the roots, is *of* people more than it is *for* people, and which facilitates the asking of tough questions about life and death in the light of the Christian faith. Above all, attempts at being in Christ through the Spirit – in communities of mission and ministry – should enable self knowledge, the knowledge of God, and ever deeper relationships with all creation.

In making plans for the Church our aim should be to integrate the quest for holiness with the best available contemporary wisdom about the management of ministry. Neglect of good management is to fail to love people enough. It is this requirement that we should be proud of the Church we are – because its proclamation and practice attempt to echo the triune God's life and love – that provides the impetus for drawing together disparate elements of a challenging new culture of Church into a coherent but flexible strategy, depending on local history, theology, culture and personalities.

Over the past twenty years I have found inspiration by keeping informed of the international and ecumenical debate concerning an ecclesiology rooted in the concept of communion which in many parts of the world has evolved into some form of Local Ministry. There is in this book an underlying commitment to the view that for the next period of the Church of England's development a key element in its strategy for mission and ministry in the parishes will be the creation and nurturing of Local Ministry Teams. Precisely what I mean by this, and what will be the most appropriate terminology to use, I will discuss as the argument unfolds. For now I refer the reader to six helpful points of definition of Local Ministry identified at a national Consultation sponsored by the Edward King Institute for Ministry Development in 1994:

1. There is a biblical and theological imperative for collaborative ministry. It is not just a current fashion or a response to crisis.
2. Ministry belongs to the whole people of God by virtue of their baptism into Christ.
3. There is a common calling to all God's people to share in the service (ministry) of their local church.

4. The local church is the universal Church present in each locality.
5. The trinitarian understanding of God and the theology of the Body of Christ point to a community of diversity in which all are entrusted with a ministry of costly reconciliation.
6. The role of the ordained ministry is to serve and service the whole ministry of the people of God.

The Edward King Institute consultation followed the principle of beginning by learning from the many experiences of those present, then identifying elements of good practice which apply to different approaches, leading to the working out of a theological critique and rationale. To honour that approach in this book I begin in Chapter One by setting out the experience of Local Ministry in the Church of England and commend one model in particular, developed especially in Lincoln and Gloucester. Chapter Two examines the importance of a theology of place, community and mission. In Chapter Three I identify the doctrine of the Trinity as a key to interpreting the concept of community and the quality of human relationships. The need to define the role of the parish priest, together with other clergy and Readers is explored in Chapter Four. Chapter Five examines urgent issues about power sharing that must be faced if the meaning and reality of collaboration is to come to light. The final chapter sums up the argument in reasserting good practice in local ministry strategies.

My own credentials for writing on this theme include the following. In the 1980s I was involved in developing a Local Ministry Scheme in Ripon Diocese and was parish priest of Halton, Leeds, in which, at that time Local Ministry seemed to the committed congregation a natural development of our experiments in collaborative ministry. The Spirit constantly offers the invitation to move on, to reassess and reform. Experience revealed how those early ideas lacked a true local flexibility. For nine years I was part of the resource team for the parishes in Gloucester Diocese. There it seemed that a strategy, rather than a single model, of Local Ministry should be the proper vehicle for focusing new developments in shared mission and ministry. In my present work as Ministry Development Officer in the Diocese of Chelms-ford I am in a position both to observe and share in stimulating continuing developments in the theology and practice of the Diocese and the wider Church.

I ⚹ LOCAL MINISTRY IN PRACTICE

New Strategies for Ministry in the Local Church

Church life at present lurches from despair to messianism. One moment all seems to be hopeless – the old familiar securities are gone – or else someone proposes a remedy for all ills. To claim that a key element in the mission and ministry of the local church of the future is the development of Local Ministry may seem to be falling into the latter category. I hope, however, to show how this proposed strategy is capable of gathering up many strands of current thinking – a single strategy with many local outcomes. In practice the majority of the dioceses of the Church of England have adopted some form of Local Ministry, often embracing experiments in collaborative ministry which have been in evidence for at least twenty–five years. In the Roman Catholic Church worldwide there is an increasing commitment to the training of laity as pastors, teachers and eucharistic ministers (Kerkhofs 1995).

In the Church of England varying models of Local Ministry exist side by side, with overlapping and unique characteristics. Co-ordination has been difficult, partly because of the autonomy of bishops and dioceses and also because the concept draws together previously separated councils and boards for mission, ministry and education. A particularly fruitful way forward now is for a diocese to have an all-embracing Resource Team with a single Council answerable to the Bishop's Council and Synod. Diocesan schemes vary in how they envisage the collaborative involvement of laity in general, Readers in particular, and clergy, whether stipendiary or not. In different places the concept of Local Ministry, the processes of selection, training, accreditation, terms of service, maintenance, and links with the rest of the Church all vary considerably, as the literature on the schemes bears out. There are also differing agendas, whether the ministry is in a rural, suburban or urban area, or in recognition of varying intellectual opportunities, abilities, social confidence and learning styles. This latter issue is extremely complex and patronizing assumptions about learning abilities need to be scrupulously avoided. Another vital question lies with the extent of the responsibilities of a given Local Ministry team, say in relation to the roles and authority of the parish priest or Parochial Church Council.

Schemes vary too in the emphasis placed on the ministry of the whole congregation, the relationship between the local church and the needs of the interlocking communities that constitute the neighbourhood, and on the extent to which connections are made between worship and everyday matters in the home, workplace, community, leisure and unemployment. Much depends on the metaphors, vocabulary and concepts of mission that form the operational theology of local ministry. Although schemes in the dioceses of Guildford, Hereford, Lichfield, Liverpool, Southwark, Truro, Winchester – to name just a few – use theories, practice and language that in many ways look similar, there are underlying models which vary considerably. Although the 1992 Advisory Board of Ministry Review of Local Non-Stipendiary Schemes clearly focused on Local Non-Stipendiary Ministry (LNSM), it offers an insight into three basic models of Ministry Teams:

Model A: An integrated approach to training lay and ordained (LNSM) members for local ministry teams. All the members of the local ministry team train together and will minister together, though with distinctive responsibilities. This model could be said to characterize the Lincoln Scheme for local ministry.

Model B: The training of ordinands for LNSM, within local groups which are not local ministry teams. Ordinands and lay people train together for some elements within the ordinands' training, but the purpose of these groups is not to equip the lay members to exercise a Church-based lay ministry. This model could be said to characterize the approach of the Diocese of Truro.

Model C: The training only of ordinands for LNSM, where the training takes place in diocesan groups with other ordinands for LNSM. The training is based upon groups but the groups do not contain those preparing for lay ministry or undertaking lay education. The dioceses which have used this model, namely Southwark and Manchester, both have separate but well-developed programmes of lay education and lay training already in existence.

Several national consultations have revealed the development of a greater complexity of models. Not all of them can be greeted with equal enthusiasm. It must be the work of another study to present detailed descriptions of the range of diocesan schemes, analysing their similarities and differences. Space does not allow for this here. There were numerous references at the Edward King Institute 1994 Consultation to 're-inventing the wheel'. Lessons learnt in one diocese seemed to be ignored or not known about by others. There is no mechanism in the Church of England by which dioceses can learn from each other in this field. This is partly because although this initiative is clearly about new ministerial arrangements, it is no less about a radical and hopeful initiative in mission, evangelism and spirituality at the grass roots of the church. Specific recommendations that emerged from the Consultation were:

(a) The establishment of a national collection of resource material for Local Ministry training, put together in a way that shows different theological and educational approaches.

(b) The setting up of a national project to identify and disseminate good practice in Local Ministry.

(c) The regional integration of ministerial training resources, which would bring together initial ministerial training, training for Local Ministry, continuing ministerial education and the continuing education of local ministerial teams.

As a temporary measure, the Diocese of Gloucester Local Ministry Office is currently building up an information bank on local ministry schemes across the country and on the strategy of other dioceses. Further information is always welcome.

It seems very clear that there is great urgency to keep checking that the models of local ministry which are being adopted are adequate in their theological assumptions as well as in their ability to deliver appropriate strategies for collaborative mission and ministry. It is vital also to safeguard participants from inadequately considered strategies and from the notorious swings of parish direction associated with the succession of parish priests. Of course, an incoming priest has the apostolic task to discern what may need redirecting, but so often the work of the laity is totally dishonoured in these circumstances. There are tragically too many stories of lack of faithfulness to the hard work and insight of parishes between one priest and another to let this go without making the point very strongly.

It would have been all too easy to begin this book with theological theories. However, to make contact immediately with members of Local Ministry Teams and parishes where this is practised in one form or another, I shall begin by a detailed description of the model of Local Ministry which I favour as most appropriate. This is in no way to suggest there must be identical practice and vocabulary in every place. Rather, I believe that in response to the drift of this strategy there can evolve whole clusters of particular outworkings according to context.

A Model of Local Ministry

Local Ministry will not work unless it is energetically adopted as a key part of the strategy of a diocese. Given the constraints of budgeting, staffing levels and the many calls on the energy of bishops, archdeacons and training officers, it will not flourish where it is not embraced wholeheartedly. Fundamentally, if this Local Ministry strategy fails to deliver the next generation of patterns of mission and ministry, what alternatives are realistically available? The diocesan scheme in Gloucester, which I helped to establish gradually over most of a decade, is a response to enthusiasm and experimentation in parishes about collaborative ministry. However, it did not develop without considerable work in teaching and discussion of the theological principles underlying the nature of the Church and its sharing in God's mission, which have been the subject of international ecumenical debate since the middle of the twentieth century.

Through this strategy the diocese offers support and guidance on good practice to parishes keen either to start Local Ministry from scratch or to review and revise an informal or parish-sponsored experiment in collaborative ministry. It is a very practical way of encouraging the people and clergy of the diocese to rediscover and develop their joint ministries. The vision of this strategy is that each local church be enabled to look confidently to the future with a healthy ministry of word, sacrament, pastoral care, evangelism, social concern, and transformation of the neighbourhood – the whole range of missionary tasks.

It is my understanding of a diocesan Local Ministry scheme that it will enable the selection, training and authorizing of teams of lay and ordained people for ministry in the local church and community. But it is far more than that; it is a long-term vision for parish development and witness. It signals the end of an era in which the ministry of clergy – even 'helped' by laity – was supreme. Now it is possible to say that there is no need of polarities – either clergy or laity. Both together, equally in partnership, are being called by God for mission and ministry in and through the local church. While a scheme which includes vocations to Local Non-Stipendiary Ministry needs the national recognition of the Advisory Board of Ministry and the House of Bishops as providing training to nationally acceptable standards, it must be recognized as designed to respond extremely flexibly to the needs and circumstances of each different parish, benefice, team, and deanery involved.

The model of Local Ministry which I find most appropriate is a reframing of concepts of ministry, not an attempt merely to bolster up what has served in the past. In a time of transition, the best fruits of the past are brought through in the strategies of the new. The Gloucester scheme, devised in dialogue with previous developments in the Diocese of Lincoln, is offered as a positive step in reclaiming an understanding of how to be Church. Resonating with the vision of church members considered as interactive musicians in an orchestra led by clergy of vision (Warren 1995), Local Ministry puts into practice the world-wide rediscovery in most main-line churches of the ministry of all believers. It includes:

- the belief that through baptism God calls each person to ministry
- the belief that God gives to his Church the gifts that it needs to be the church in a particular place.

The Gloucester Scheme

The launch of the scheme in Gloucester was the culmination of almost a decade of debate and experiment in the Diocese. Beginning with a response to the *Tiller Report* and *Lima* documents, and including *Faith in the City, Faith in the Countryside*, and varied local responses, people explored how to cater for the changing needs for lay and ordained ministry working in collaboration. At first there was both passionate enthusiasm and opposition. Only half the parishes would even admit to having discussed a strategy document agreed at diocesan Synod. In due time the Local Ministry Scheme was recognized, not as one bright idea among many, nor just as a way of facing a crisis, but as a carefully considered way forward involving the entire diocese. It is probably true that had there been no problems with staffing and money, it is unlikely that the idea of Local Ministry would in itself have been so attractive. While declining numbers of stipendiary clergy and financial stringency mean a reassessment of the way the Church offers ministry, Local Ministry is nevertheless not just a response to decline. Some have called it 'God's left hand at work'. It is positively stimulated by the patterns of ministry in the New Testament and the first rather than the second millennium of the Church's history (see Schillebeeckx 1985) and is in line with world-wide contemporary developments. Two years into the full practice of the Gloucester diocesan scheme the results are extremely encouraging and bring a sense of following the lead of the Holy Spirit.

The essence of a Local Ministry Team is that it involves lay and ordained working together. It offers a powerhouse of prayer and energy, vision and direction to lead and enable the ministry of the local church. It links the local with the diocesan and the wider Church. The specific roles undertaken by each team are different and will change over the course of the life of the team – as changes occur in the membership as well as in the character of the local church itself. All teams work both with the congregation and wider community, and are there to enable the ministry of others, to lead where appropriate, and above all to help others explore their own faith and grow. On a regular basis team members are asked to teach others what they have recently learnt.

Team members must serve no more than three terms of office so the team naturally evolves and regenerates.

The basic steps followed by a parish or benefice hoping to form a team are as follows:

1. Teaching and exploring at every point of congregation and parish life what is meant today by the mission of the local church through its entire membership in the whole of their lives. This is reinforced through the encouragement of everyone to grow through nourishing worship, a policy of inclusiveness, and dedication to study, prayer, spiritual direction and growth (see Gill 1994).

2. Careful discussions take place between one of the Diocesan Local Ministry Officers (LMO) and parish priest and Parochial Church Council (PCC) to explore what the scheme can offer and whether it might be right in that place at that time. Open meetings and letters to houses in the parishes explain the idea to as many people as possible. As the wider public will be exposed to new ministerial arrangements at baptisms, weddings, and funerals, for example, it is vital that every effort be made to inform them of these developments. Members of the church's fringe will read magazine articles, may attend a parish meeting called for the purpose, or receive a general flyer to all residents, or be interested to read local press reports. This part of the process – consulting local residents – has enormous potential for increasing mutual understanding and communication between church and neighbourhood.

3. The parish or benefice undertakes a short study course entitled *Exploring Local Ministry*. The course is led by lay and ordained people from the parish based on material supplied by the diocese. This includes an 'audit' of the church and explains in more detail how the Local Ministry Scheme works and the forms it can take. At the end, if they want to proceed further, the PCC may ask the bishop for permission to begin to form a team. At all stages the Local Ministry Officer works closely with parish(es) to support and advise as well as to represent the bishop and diocese in their plans.

4. Members of the local church and community are asked to

nominate people for inclusion in the team. Preparatory preaching and teaching about the nature of vocation, discernment and the nature of the Church is important, as is a clear understanding about what it is that the parish is trying to establish. All Readers and Non-Stipendiary Ministers are automatically part of the team.

5. When all nominations are in, the PCC meets in the course of worship and silence, individually and in confidence to consider the list of names, marking each as a 'Yes', or 'No', or 'I don't know enough about this person to judge'. The Local Ministry Officer and parish priest together study the PCC contribution to the process and draw up a list of those to be asked – with one or two reserves. The parish priest may nominate team members; his right of veto over names proposed may only be used after careful discussion with the LMO. When the team has been formed, Local Ministry is formally launched in the benefice with a Commissioning Service led by a bishop. It is the parish and not the team members themselves that is accredited and blessed in this new venture. All the people of the parish or benefice are commissioned for Local Ministry, to be led by the team which will develop that total ministry.

The diocese provides structured support and training over the first two-and-a-half years of the life of the team. To reinforce the collaborative nature of local ministry, clergy take part in team learning. Each team works with a tutor – an experienced lay or ordained minister from outside the parish – to guide them through the early days of working at collaborative ministry. The number of available tutors can be increased through running training courses. It is particularly important that tutors should understand the different learning styles and needs of team members and be aware of their own preference so that they consciously make room for others. In addition to meeting together to discuss parish business, teams work on four five-week training modules each year. In a typical year, two modules offer background (e.g. Old Testament, New Testament, Pastoral care, Ethics, Worship, etc.); one is a practical project involving other members of the congregation and community; one gives the opportunity for each team member to specialize. Personal specialism courses are held each year all over the diocese by experts in their own field. Each team member takes a member from their congregation on the course with them. In the autumn of 1994 over 300 people from Local Ministry parishes in Gloucester Diocese followed courses ranging from All-age worship, the meaning of the Eucharist, to caring for the dying and bereaved, or running an after school club. It is vital that the team is recognized as enabling the whole church membership in education and training, rather than as on the old model of the priesthood, ministering on behalf of everyone else. Otherwise Local Ministry Teams would be a re-invention of clericalism, feeding dependency and setting up powerful and exclusive cliques among the laity.

Continuous assessment is an integral part of the scheme, and also regular review with team, parish, parish priest, tutor and LMO. When a team is authorized by the Bishop after two years in existence, a rolling programme of Continuing Ministerial Training (CME) and Team Review begins. Teams are formally reviewed every three years and licences renewed in the same way as for Readers.

Keeping a clear and healthy relationship between the team and the PCC is extremely important. The scheme helps a PCC lay the foundations of a vision for the team but the fine-detail can only be worked out between the team and the PCC over a period of time. Many team members are often also PCC members but there is also a formal process of reporting back to the PCC on what the team is achieving and experiencing.

At any point in the process the team may suggest ordination to an individual or an individual may propose consideration of their own vocation to ordained ministry. In the case of candidates for Local Non-Stipendiary Ministry (LNSM) who have arisen from the team, the PCC is asked if they support the candidacy before the normal diocesan selection process can begin. If a candidate is selected he or she undertakes additional training whilst remaining a fully integrated member of the team.

Some of the Benefits

In the process of debate leading up to the establishing of the

Gloucester Scheme eight advantages were identified as significant:

(i) There is provision in the scheme for a general continuity between successive parish clergy. As I noted earlier, all too often the history of parishes has been 'written' in parallel with the arrival and departure of parish priests. It seems vital now that any clergy considering becoming vicar of a parish should respect the agenda and work of the local people – even though part of the apostolic role of the parish priest will be not only to affirm but to challenge and develop it. This is an issue about the wider Church keeping faith with local people as well as the local church being open to the diocese and wider Church.

(ii) Whatever the degree of formality in a diocese, a scheme makes it possible for the bishop, through his officers, to ask rigorous questions about the process of selection of Local Ministry Teams.

(iii) A similar point can be made regarding both initial formation and on-going training, bearing in mind the importance of membership changing and evolving over even quite a few years.

(iv) Through the diocesan scheme it is *parishes* which are commissioned, *not individual team members*. Local Ministry is about providing a means for the ministerial growth of *the whole Church*, not about the commissioning of some laity for ministry to the exclusion of others. Yes, it requires a team with evolving membership but never as a neo-clerical substitute for the work of others for God's Kingdom.

(v) There would also be provision for effecting the dignified retirement of members after the serving of an agreed term or on other grounds. There is a rolling programme of retirement and renewal.

(vi) A range of ministries which the clergy can no longer handle can be not only maintained, but strengthened and expanded.

(vii) Within the scheme, vocations to ordination can be encouraged and vocation in the world explored more deeply.

(viii) An orthodox, well reasoned, theology of mission and ministry in touch with the worldwide Church is enacted and reflected upon.

The Local Ministry Officers in Gloucester have been tremendously encouraged by the continued high level of interest in the scheme and the results already to be seen in parishes and benefices with teams. Team membership spans the age range from teens to 70s with the average in their late 40s. Occupations of team members already include the following: nurse, youth worker, teacher, estate manager, doctor, secretary, mechanic, housewife, farmer, post office worker, car salesman, retail manager, courier, retired, market research interviewer, civil servant, nursery teacher, guest house proprietor, and young mother.

Local Ministry Develops the Faith and Confidence of Team Members

Although I want to emphasize that the Local Ministry Team is there to evoke and sustain the ministry of the entire church, experience shows already the great benefit for the team members themselves. Personal testimonies and reflections on taking part in the work of Local Ministry Teams in differing settings begin to reveal some of the rich fruits that this new development can bring to the life of the churches.

(i) One person speaks of knowing for the first time 'what God was calling me to do'. She has experienced a sense of fellowship in a very diverse group of leaders in which 'we are learning to recognize each others' gifts'.

(ii) Another writes, 'On a personal note I am more confident, my faith is strengthened and I am much more aware, not only of needs within the parish, but also on a wider scale.' Membership of a Local Ministry Team for some has brought a focused and disciplined opportunity to engage in mission – expressed in hospital and sick visiting, preparing families before and visiting after a baptism or funeral, or helping to reflect on issues in the workplace – linked with an expectation that such ministries will be rooted in prayer and carefully supervised. None of this has happened easily or quickly and has often required patience as others have been slow to recognize the positive benefits. Moving from the older models of mission and ministry to this one can meet painful resistance.

(iii) Others tell of how earlier experiments were very much about 'helping' the tired and overstretched clergy – in hospital visiting, assisting at baptism and funerals and in the pastoral visits involved. The Local Ministry Scheme moves beyond this stage to empowering every person equally, but differently, for collaborative responsibility. Team members themselves can take some convincing that they are not in ministry at the mere goodwill of the clergy. For this reason the term 'pastoral assistant' is unhelpful. In the first place this expression limits lay ministry to pastoral work rather than opening it to the whole rainbow of possible parish ministries. Second, it suggests that laity are merely helpers of the clergy – 'assistants' rather than colleagues with specific but parallel ministries.

(iv) Other testimonies speak of the transformative power of Local Ministry as it provides training and spiritual development as a vehicle for a 'bubbly excitement' about the new possibilities for clergy and laity in local mission together.

(v) The laughter and good spirits at local ministry training events speaks volumes. Local Ministry clearly promotes lay confidence, widening vision, deepening faith, the chance for many to have spiritual direction, and the invitation to take a lead in the local church without being thought presumptuous or interfering.

The Testimony of a Tutor to a Local Ministry Team

I have been a tutor for a local ministry team covering two villages. Just this week we finished our first module of 'Caring for People'. The team presented their group assignment which was meant to include a commitment to some sort of visiting. I was dumbstruck – a fact which caused them great amusement! Their visiting project was a comprehensive analysis of all the principal categories of visiting in the parishes, with background, prioritized tasks, realistic (slightly optimistic) timetable, criteria for measuring success and finally a list of what they had already achieved to date. It represented a truly awesome amount of work, both in its preparation and in its implementation – and they were serious in what they were intending to do.

Clearly the tutor was humbled. As a recently ordained priest, though with former mission experience as a layman, he was energized by their enthusiasm, discipline and commitment. He rightly questions whether as working people they could or should maintain such momentum. Local Ministry could take up too much of people's time. It may be helpful to keep checking out the full range of roles that any member should be fulfilling as a human being as well as a local church minister, for example as parent, spouse, son or daughter, worker, home manager, school governor, as well as a human being with a need for space and time alone as well as with others outside the church.

Local Ministry as the Focus for New Developments in Mission and Ministry

For effective Local Ministry, theology and spirituality need to become as important as fabric maintenance and initiatives for the Church to become self-financing. In the 1970s there was great optimism about the development of a theologically rooted Christian community in the local church:

> When the history of the Church in our times is written, perhaps the most significant revolution will have been the rediscovery of ministry within community, the ministry of disciples to one another, the prophetic expectation, the courage and joy to believe, hope, and love for one another in his name and power. (Farrell 1974)

In reality many local churches glimpse some elements of this vision, but it is unusual to find many in one place. A strategy for Local Ministry offers precisely what is needed here. It is common experience in the Church of England that it can be hard to move discussion away from the pragmatic to a theological consideration of aims and strategies. However, in reality a long campaign is being waged to determine the nature of the Church of England. Will it continue to be committed to the entire neighbourhood or pursue the easier goal of congregationalism? Too easily we speak in terms of opposing polarities – 'If this is the age of the laity then are the clergy redundant?' 'If the laity are in ministry we don't need clergy to preside at the Eucharist!' This polarizing tendency completely misses the point. Dare the ever pragmatic Church of England work out an understanding of the Church that gives equal value to clergy and laity, though recognizing differences in role and opportunity? Local Ministry has most chance of a healthy future where there is a clear vision of a new way of being Church which is articulated and owned by a large proportion of the worshipping community.

A key feature of any Local Ministry arrangements requires a change in the ministerial style and approach of the stipendiary clergy. Local Ministry requires clergy who can be open to developing collaborative ministry, who are willing to take risks and are not afraid of failure. Their skills in listening, managing change and resources, assessment and consultancy, review and oversight, will also be much in demand. It is widely accepted that many of the present parish priests perceived their vocation and were selected with a quite different role in mind. Processes of selection and initial training as well as in-service training all now need to recognize the different ideals and skills that a priest will require. The training of stipendiary clergy along with new teams of which they are members and leaders, must be recognized as a vital procedure, both for bonding and for the signals it gives to the local church and all concerned.

The local church, never in isolation from the wider Church (geographically, historically, and theologically), must recognize that ministry is the work of the entire Church. All the baptized have gifts to bring to the mission of the local church that calls each one (see Lumen Gentium 17 and 35). A balance of local initiative and diocesan support can offer appropriate training and encouragement to enable the local church to fulfil its task of being a missionary community. An external tutor, supervisor or 'team friend' acting as consultant and enabler for the training can focus the proper tension between parish and diocese.

Local Ministry Teams need simple, clear, known and owned lines of accountability. This is partly a consequence of the PCC and parish owning the idea of a team, theologically and pragmatically. Teams need to meet for their own nurturing, education, and spiritual development, not just for administrative purposes. Leadership and ministry are not synonymous, and clear boundaries must be drawn between the work of the team and the PCC. The team may well have vision and energy for discerning new directions in parish life, but decision-making must remain firmly with the PCC. Readers should be firmly recognized as part of any existing team. Local answers must be found for questions regarding the liturgical and preaching roles of specific team members and regarding the length of tenure of team members.

Conclusion

'Local' can be summarized in two ways. *First, it is a unit that is able to sustain and work with a visible team of people. Second, it is the scale on which it is possible for people to relate person to person.*

Local Ministry may be defined in essence as *shared* or *collaborative* ministry. For most members of the Edward King Institute 1994 Consultation, the term 'Local Ministry' implied 'Local Ministry Teams'. One group described local ministry as 'laity and clergy working together, making decisions together, praying together, training together, and supporting one another creatively and critically'. The concept of a partnership of ordained and lay is integral to the idea of Local Ministry.

An important emphasis must be that ministry teams are constituted of people of different gifts, skills, temperaments and methods, not just the like minded. The Consultation also stressed the need for the development of a common vision within each team, recognizing that this requires 'wide discussion of and agreement on values and purpose'.

Another aspect of Local Ministry is its *contextual* nature. Local Ministry is rooted in the reality of the local community. Members of the Consultation were particularly conscious of the differences between urban and rural communities and emphasized they cannot be treated alike. Many dioceses have higher degrees of obvious deprivation than Gloucester and later I shall explore more of how Local Ministry can be a vital way of the Church being open to those for whom everyday circumstances offer little hope. A number of groups at the Consultation pinpointed the need for greater contextual elements in the formation and training of Local Ministry Teams.

This emphasis on the contextual nature of Local Ministry reflects its task and mission. One group described the task of the Local Ministry Team as 'enabling the local church to discover how it is called to make God visible in the local community, and then doing it'. Another said 'Local Ministry is directed to the community and not just to the church. Hence it needs a form appropriate to this community'. Identifying the needs and resources of the local community in order to be part of redeeming or transforming them is a key element in Local Ministry.

I have stressed already the importance of beginning this discussion about Local Ministry as the key to the Church's mission and ministry strategy with accounts of real experience. We are free now to begin exploring some of the big ideas in theology that undergird this practice and without which it will founder, as merely crisis management bolted on to ailing structures.

2 ℂ A THEOLOGY OF THE LOCAL CHURCH

In a mission-orientated church in which many realize that in a wide variety of ways they have a part to play, the vision needs to be owned by the congregation. It can be observed that new experiments with ministry teams in the dioceses take root much more effectively when care has been taken to sink deep theological foundations through patient and thorough dialogical teaching. The end result can be the articulation of a common theology of Church, allowing for the particular vocabularies that differing traditions within the churches will favour and understand.

There is an increasing recognition today that theology cannot be just communicated by one person speaking to another or rolled out like a motorway in every place the same. Theological ideas evolve systemically – as issues, personalities, events and needs interact. Think, if you will, of a huge wheel with a hub and spokes as a way of showing how the systemic forces of a theology of Church (ecclesiology) all affect each other. In the hub of this wheel lies the profound New Testament concept of *koinonia*, communion. I will draw out its significance later. The 'spokes' of the wheel of a theology of Church represent these interrelated issues: the renewed understanding of ministry in the New Testament communities, the recognition of baptism as the main clue to mission and ministry, the seminal contribution of Vatican II, the Lima documents, and theologians who have expounded and developed that significance, a new general awareness of the importance of being deliberately open to the Holy Spirit, the rediscovery of the significance of the trinitarian understanding of God's being, the Church as a mirror of God's triune life, the eucharistic centre to the life of the local church, the need to be open to the local context, and the importance of an eschatological view of the life of the Church. These will be opened up as the book continues.

Here in this second chapter I want to emphasize the indigenous character of local mission and ministry by picking out the spokes of the 'wheel' of context, issues about place, community and mission.

The Whole of the Church in Every Place

It is a key concept in this book that the local church, which has at its heart the celebration of the Eucharist, contains in microcosm the entire world Church. The local church may have several differently constituted worshipping congregations at various times in a week or month. For Anglicans such assemblies will hold Christians of widely differing theological views and on a wide spectrum of spiritual journeys.

'How local is "local"?' must be a pressing question in days of pastoral re-organization. Cities reveal a determination of some worshippers to pass the door of many churches to find one that is congenial. In the countryside on Sundays although drivers will travel many miles to supermarkets and DIY stores, a characteristic of rural Anglican congregations is the maintenance of a loyalty to that building which is in the settlement where they live, often opposing attempts to close buildings or to create a workable 'local church' from several mediaeval parishes.

Areas of Collaborative Ministry

My own vision for the future that is emerging, in response to all the factors mentioned already, is of local churches that take in very wide swathes of territory, so that inherited ministerial arrangements, already under review, will continually need adjustment. The parish system with its many buildings must now be secondary to the redevelopment of the *idea* of the local church as a locally negotiated area of collaborative ministry. If particular buildings remain viable and are in appropriate locations they may continue to have their place, but vision and pragmatic issues together will be questioning the rightness of more than one church building of any denomination in each geographical community. I reflect here on my experience as a diocesan officer of arriving in a village on a Sunday morning to preside or preach at the Eucharist to find a short line of cars outside the Anglican parish church and just up the road a similar line parked outside the Methodist church. How long can this really continue? What connection has this with shelves of ecumenical texts and declarations produced in the past two decades?

In close collaboration with the diocesan bishop, groups of former parishes and deaneries should be enabled to group themselves, with ecumenical co-operation, into the most appropriate 'local churches'. The diocese and local communities, working together, can then begin to see how a relatively small number of stipendiary clergy can lead the mission of the local church in partnership with other clergy (NSM, LNSM, and retired), Readers, Local Ministry Teams and laity with many gifts. Acting as a theological and leadership resource, a stipendiary priest – or at least a priest who is available throughout the week – will have oversight of this new development. One of the results of this process should be the development of a new kind of autonomy in relatedness which will go some way towards healing the division between the central and the local, the diocese and the parish.

Theologically, the communion of Christians is rooted not only in the sacraments, word and local fellowship, but in the ministry of the episcopate. For Anglicans the Lambeth Quadrilateral includes the episcopate as well as the sacraments, together with the apostolic faith revealed in Scripture and articulated in the creeds. If we are to talk in terms of centres at all, it is best that each local church should consider the Church to be two-eyed. Yes, of course where the bishop has his seat will be an important place, but theologically and spiritually, *wherever* there is a local mission and local Eucharist, there also the world Church has a 'centre'. In a Church that stops scapegoating one part of itself it may even be possible to recognize that God has given an equal responsibility of caring for the whole Church to everyone. There is a sense in which all Christians are bishops – all share in the episcopal office which for practical reasons is focused in certain individuals. All are called. No one is redundant.

A Church which Celebrates and Hears Many Local Cultures

The agenda of the local church must always be to *include* rather than *exclude*. Unconsciously churches reject large tracts of humanity by failing to make provision for them to find a 'space' which they can occupy without automatically denying their culture, music, way of speech, or capacity to handle texts and concepts. It is all too easy for one priest or even a powerful group of laity to ensure that the local church runs on the resources (and with the limitations) that only they can see or offer. What is mission if not the engagement with God in the entire enterprise of bringing the whole of creation to its intended destiny? A local church cannot claim to be part of this if it fails to work with all ages, if it only serves itself, or if it operates entirely on a Radio 4 model to the exclusion of all else. This is another reason for no one being in ministry alone. One person offering ministry to a community will usually be unable to react with more than a couple of cultural groups – like a lighthouse that only shines out through a tiny window, leaving all the rest of the circumference of its tower in darkness. A team can shine in many different directions at once, attracting a wide range of responses in the neighbourhood.

There are so many ways of serving God's Kingdom which other networks in a neighbourhood will be involved in. When we use the word 'church' we need to be careful to think beyond the events on Sunday morning in church. Like the ebb and flow of the sea, the local church can choose to place equal emphasis on its gathering for worship, study and fellowship and on its being separated and exposed to the world's needs through every member. There are also many different modes of operation which have to be chosen. I was impressed on a visit to the Province of Kenya by often very poor churches (in financial terms) that engaged in mission across a whole spectrum: in the provision of a clinic, a school, AIDS counselling, help with loans, training in the use of sewing machines, as well as evangelism, worship and lay training. Parishes that move towards becoming areas of collaborative ministry – in terms not unlike those in the Tiller Report which was so feared when published in 1983 – could between them offer a wide variety of religious experience as well as of teaching, outreach and social concern.

There are many parts of Britain – for example, vast derelict housing estates – where the Church needs to abandon paternalistic church *for* people attitudes. Local Ministry can say to those who have been institutionalized into poor self-esteem, 'You are a royal priesthood, you are God's people, you are precious in

God's sight.' As *Faith in the City* still reminds the churches, there is a gospel-shaped task in a society whose interests are at odds with the poorest of its members. Where people have internalized a low self-image, where relationships are so profoundly dysfunctional, and where isolation rather than communion is the key, the local church has special opportunities. Instead of reinforcing people's notions of being no good to anyone, Local Ministry has the potential to cut through apathy and offer constructive resources for personal and community development. To professional ministers and dependent congregations this will feel awfully risky. But what is there to lose? Local Ministry can offer liturgies, education, the practice of ministry, hope and creativity by encouraging the involvement of all and celebrating the inclusion of those the world prefers to leave behind.

A holistic local church will make provision for thought and feelings, idea and picture, concept and narrative, and uniqueness held in kaleidoscopic variety. In pictorial terms it is like a round church building with walls entirely made of doors – draughty perhaps, but overflowing with people.

A Theology Rooted in 'Communion'

There is rightly a good deal of suspicion about what the word 'community' means. It always needs a qualifying word. In Christians terms it is something about the quality and the nature of the relatedness that flows between God and humanity and between one person and another in church and neighbourhood.

The Fruits of International Ecumenical Debate

Through prayer and study together, Anglicans and Roman Catholics in the past decade have found the New Testament term *koinonia* (communion) to be a vital key to understanding the nature of the Church (Avis 1990). In the *Final Report* of ARCIC I and the statement *Salvation and the Church* of ARCIC II, *communion* was offered as a basic building block of a theology of Church (ecclesiology). ARCIC II then proceeded to make a full consideration of *communion* as the life-giving work of God. *Communion* as a central Old Testament theme is revealed in the unfolding of narratives showing how God takes the initiative in inviting humanity – created in his likeness – into relationship, followed by the breakdown and renewal of this relationship (Gen. 12.1–3; Exod.19.5–6; Deut. 12.5; Jer. 31.31ff.; Isa. 49.6; Mic. 4.1–4). The New Testament portrays God restoring the broken relationship through his Son and the company of those with whom he shares his mission. In the power of the Spirit, the baptizing communities witness to the restoration of communion with Father, Son and Spirit, through the ministry, death and resurrection of Jesus.

Sharing in Holy Communion makes Community

The Eucharist (or Holy Communion or the Mass) becomes the focus for participating in this renewed relationship in the body of Christ. Communion with the Father, through the Son, in the Holy Spirit actually makes the Church, the people of the New Covenant. The Easter mystery creates a communion in which all human barriers become meaningless and relationship between humanity and creation is restored (Col. 1.15–20; Gal. 3.27–29). Through the continuing working of the reconciliation made possible in Christ, in the sacramental life of the church, the human damage done to *communion* can be healed (Matt. 18.15–20). The New Testament recognizes the tension between the sinfulness of disciples and the hope of the perfection of creation. The celebration of the Eucharist is a first taste of that peace which will come at the end of all things. Sharing the peace liturgically can be a powerfully effective symbol of the local Christian community pledging itself once again to allowing itself to be used by God as a vehicle for bringing in the kingdom values of the gospel – through the everyday acts and relationships of church and neighbourhood.

In the New Testament *koinonia* draws together a cluster of primary ideas – unity, life together, sharing at deep levels. Essentially to describe church as 'communion' is to speak of a network of relationships rooted in sharing a single reality. So, 'Because there is one loaf, we, though many, are one body; for it is one loaf of which we all partake' (1 Cor. 10.17) or 'in order that you may share with us in a common life, that life which we share with the Father and his Son Jesus Christ' (1 John 1.3). Communion is the idea undergirding the phrases which evoke the common life of the Church – people of God, flock, vine, temple, bride, and body of Christ – in which a relationship with Christ implies a relationship with all others who are in him. Sharing in the life of the Trinity, through Christ in the Holy Spirit, makes us one with fellow Christians. Paul's imagery in 1 Corinthians further draws out that these organic relationships are created and sustained sacramentally through baptism and the presence of the Risen Christ in the eucharistic assembly and sharing of bread and wine.

Helping the World to Grow up in the Form of Christ

To be in Christ through the Spirit is to share in a human fellowship of teaching, Eucharist and prayer, which suffers with Christ as it looks to his final glorification, 'My one desire is to know Christ and the power of his resurrection, and to share his sufferings in growing conformity with his death, in hope of somehow attaining the resurrection from the dead' (Phil. 3.10f.). This is a community of mutual serving in joy and sorrow (2 Cor. 1: 6-7) and of an intimate sharing, materially and spiritually, enabled by relationship with Christ (Rom. 15.26f., 2 Cor. 8.1–15). The pastoral epistles and 1 Corinthians 11.17–34 indicate that the early churches experienced the need to structure and discipline this life of communion. The final form of communion will be known when at the end of all things creation is drawn together in Christ (Eph. 1.10).

The ARCIC II statement on Church as Communion points to the significance of the incarnate Christ as in himself the first sign of the transformed creation. It illustrates the New Testament insistence that the Christian community finds nourishment through the Spirit in living as a fellowship of believers, through the act of baptism, of participating in the bread and cup of the Eucharist, in order to be an effective instrument and sign of the coming consummation of creation. In its own life of communion, the Church witnesses to new life in Christ as a promise to the world of God's ability to overcome the destructive divisions of human sin (Eph. 2.14–18). The Church – in proclaiming the Word of God, celebrating the sacraments and pastoral care, is called to be an 'effective sign' of how the world's alienation can be overcome. The obvious failures of the Church in the past and present are not a final statement because of the promise of Christ's presence (Matt. 18.20). Paradoxically, it is in vulnerability, as a community of sinners, that the Church most clearly reveals the power of God's grace working through the one who was crucified to reconcile the world to God.

The communion of the Church in Christ through the Spirit has the primary task of revealing to the world God's purpose to create a new humanity – a pledge and foretaste here and now of the ultimate fulfilment of God's purpose for all, 'from every nation, from all tribes and peoples and tongues . . . crying out with a loud voice, "Salvation belongs to our God who sits upon the throne, and to the Lamb"' (Rev. 7.9–10).

Increasingly theology and scientific disciplines remind us that the whole of creation is included in the hope of final liberty in Christ (Rom. 8.19–23). Christian hope of salvation is not limited to humanity but is one of global proportions. Humanity and the created order are in relationship as common creatures of the triune God.

Echoing the Trinity

The concept of *communion* also runs through the Church's self-understanding of itself as being maintained in the apostolic faith it preaches. The Creeds, the episcopate, and the faithful handing on of apostolic faith in successive generations and in various cultures, are all fruits of an ecclesiology of communion (ARCIC II 1990).

The ecumenical ecclesiology of communion emphasizes that its purpose is to promote spiritual communion between the baptized person and the Trinity, to bring community together through preaching, confessing, celebrating in the Eucharist, and being led by an apostolic ministry. In uniquely different canonical structures, local churches are also called together to the visible communion that is God's will. At the heart of such communities lie relationships of forbearance, tolerance, a care for mutual interest, sharing in the body of Christ, being at one with the poorest in society, and sharing gifts both spiritual and material (Acts 2.44).

The Local Church in Mission

Observing the Church in many parts of Britain today is to meet fear and anxiety that the old ways have gone and there is nothing to take their place. It is an integral part of the argument of this book that there are new places to look for hope and vision. The local church – given its power by all the elements of eucharistic celebration (word, sacrament, fellowship, openness, and leadership) – only has a point when it knowingly commits itself to share in God's mission. This is not an isolated exercise in making more Christians – to fill the pews and the collection plate. This is not a challenge to the apathy of decline in which church attendance by diminishing numbers is little more than an extended wake. Rather, it is about sharing in God's passionate hope for all creation in the minutiae of local living and daily occupation. A new model of Church is being summoned to birth by a God who has shared his agenda of hope with humanity in the Word (*Logos*) of Jesus, and the power of the Spirit in Resurrection and Pentecost. In this God the life of the world is nurtured and recreated. Nothing less than to join God in this life and death struggle will do as the agenda of each local church.

In 1992 the House of Bishops of the Church of England reaffirmed the principle of the parochial system as the basis for mission for every person and in every community. They described this mission under three headings:

- Proclamation of the gospel in worship, word, sacrament and service.
- The pastoral ministry of the Church.
- Offering access to public worship.

This episcopal statement resonates with one of the key thrusts of the late twentieth century international ecumenical debate about the nature of the Church, that a missionary church will have two focal points to its purpose:

(i) The first is to be living now the values of the Kingdom. To be Church is to be so ordered as to point unmistakably to the end-time (*eschaton*) when humanity and the whole cosmos will know fulfilment in Christ.

(ii) The second is to be shaped by a conscious discernment of and engagement with God's own mission (Bosch 1994). A local church must see itself as a sign and foretaste of what God will have when his passionate concern for all creation is satisfied. Referring to the Greek word *eschaton*, the end, theologians call the way of looking at this 'eschatology'. This is to be the first shoots, the early blossom on the bough of God's universal desire for *shalom*, peace.

Sharing the peace in the eucharistic liturgy has very little to do with celebrating the contentment and friendship of the worshippers. Rather, given the fact that a strange collection of people find their common life in Christ draws them together, the sharing of the peace is largely a commitment, against all the odds, to work for God's peace. It is inaugmented eschatology in action. Evangelism is inviting people to respond to God's free and gracious invitation to be a part of his great mission to bring all things to a good End (Eph. 1.10; Col. 1.20; 1 Cor. 15.28).

The city set on a hill, the exposed community of worshipping believers, through all its networks of pastoral care, involvement in the wider community and provision of public worship is to be an acted sign or prophetic symbol of *shalom* (J. G. Davies 1978) as 'an exemplary form of human community' (Milbank 1990).

To Know the Needs of the Neighbourhood

Churches can unintentionally become ghettos of support for the like-minded or safe havens for the moderately healthy and moderately wealthy. At the beginning of the Decade of Evangelism a parody of church exclusivism appeared in a cartoon published in the USA. In a leafy suburb the Rector stood in the church porch next to huge notice about evangelism. A well-kitted out lady declared to the priest as she shook hands at the door, 'I really can't see what all the fuss is about, Rector. I believe that everyone in this town who *ought* to be an Anglican, *already is*.'

Various kinds of liberation theology, from Asia, South America, and Africa, as well as in Britain, together with the process of mission audits, have raised important questions regarding who actually lives in the neighbourhood. Questions arise such as:

What are people here going through at the present time? What are they suffering? What do they have to celebrate? What are the important relationships? How are they maintained? What do differing groups perceive to be the history of this place? What are the cherished traditions, memories, old feuds? What is it people want most out of life? What seem to be the most pressing issues that will affect the future of the settlement in the next decade? What is the role of the church here in contributing to the consoling, encouraging, healing, and growth in maturity of this community of communities?

This contribution to the entire neighbourhood will need to be reflected in the church community itself. Churches in both urban and rural environments share the malaise of not knowing how to survive against a backdrop of a lack of local leadership, constant struggles with money and buildings, and powerlessness to deal with the alien 'centre' where power lies. The *Faith in the City* Report looked for the development of local leadership, local churches that are outward-looking and enabling the participation of all who wish to make a contribution, with a clear ecumenical bias.

Church committees can discuss mission and evangelism for ever, but if they fail to recognize that people cannot join a community unless they are allowed in, unless 'a space' is created which they can occupy while remaining faithful to their roots, new members will find it extremely difficult to establish themselves. Unless there is a space for people of many different kinds, churches will continue to cater for a fairly narrow cross-section of the locality. In struggling to become an inclusive, comprehensive church, the analogy of the family facing decisions which will not please everyone all the time is a powerful one. Any hard-working family will know the pain of making it possible for all to have an opportunity to have their say in decision-making.

A concern for developing the mission and ministry of the local church could easily be suspected of luring the Church into introspection and a denial of its proper catholic breadth. But a church that is *merely* local or *merely* universal is not the catholic Church. Christians must be seen to have a vital role in contributing to the future of the world's development and the local church should be known and respected for its unmistakable concern for the wholeness of the entire neighbourhood.

Communities for Changing the World

So often churches in Britain limit their vision without realizing why. There are enormous advantages in engaging with the thinking of the diocese or region. A vital ingredient in knowing the task of the local church is to think globally – to engage in dialogue with creative minds from other parts of the world Church. This urgent agenda for the local church belongs to the international ecumenical debate of recent decades. Here briefly I want to witness to the power of a few of the seminal writers and texts in this field. These are some of the thinkers who (at an intellectual level) have provided much of the force behind the recent reframing of our understanding of Church.

Stanley Hauerwas

The intention of Stanley Hauerwas (an evangelical Methodist, influenced by a Mennonite while teaching in a Roman Catholic institution) was to encourage Christian communities to understand themselves as formed by the set of stories that constitute the Christian tradition (Hauerwas 1983). Narrative, tradition and local Christian community, cross-fertilizing create the organized engagement of Christ with the world today. This is reminiscent of Bonhoeffer's ecclesiology of community existing as the embodiment of Christ and in Lehmann's terms, the developing in history of the purposes of God. Concerned to remind Christians of their Jewish roots, Hauerwas describes the acted out Christian community as an alternative to the world's natural tendency – instead its fruit should be seen as living truthfully. Individually and in community Christians are to be agents of changing the world through changing oneself.

He describes this partly as a continuing dialogue between God's accusation of sin and the freedom to hear the law which hearing the Gospel makes possible. So the Church is constituted by those who hear the will of God and commit themselves to its performance. Here is the call to a journey to fulfil the calling to be holy which is made possible through God's faithfulness. This journey metaphor is linked with one of narrative. The journey is only possible for those whose existence is formed by the stories of Israel, Jesus and the Christian community. To remember and be formed by both Israel's and Jesus' stories is to be nourished as a 'contrast model' of community, a servant community which takes time to care and nurture friendships, a faithful manifestation of the peaceable Kingdom in the world, a community of peace and truth in a world of mendacity and fear, a place of hospitality to the stranger, a place of unity in a divided world, a living alternative (Hauerwas 1981, 1988). Above all, in Hauerwas we find the pivot of the Church's existence is the hope of being the firstfruits of the Kingdom so that God's will for all creation will be realized (Hauerwas 1988). I find clear reverberations here with the steely insight of the Anglican prophet Alan Ecclestone:

> The Church's real purpose should be a network of communities learning to love one another, leavening the whole populace and so transforming this devilish society we live in into something nearer the kingdom of God. (Ecclestone 1992)

Enrique Dussel

The Argentinian theologian Enrique Dussel, who has made a strong contribution to Third World ecumenical dialogue, pleads for the local church to be 'face-to-face with the poor'. Opposing the view of Christianity as a comfort to vulnerable people, Dussel suggests that in conflict with all that oppresses and diminishes persons and societies:

> The essence of the Christian life is community: being with others. This is also the essence of the reign of God: to be together with God, face-to-face with God in community. (Dussel 1988)

Advocating the praxis of the apostles (Acts 2.42–47) and the vision of *koinonia*, Dussel describes true Christian community as a celebration that takes up all relationships and all of life. The eucharistic act of sharing bread carries his understanding of a eucharistic community that works actively for the coming justice and love of God's Kingdom. The Christian community, in Dussel's understanding, exists as a sign of expectancy and anticipation. In its present practice it shares in the coming of God's reign. He dismisses prominent western theologians such as Barth, Hauerwas, Niebuhr, and Tillich for their failure to set the Church in total contrast with capitalist social and political systems. Instead he describes a subversive Christian community that looks to replace present oppressive institutions with new ones which offer the basic values of equality, justice and liberty for all (Dussel 1981). The local church as counter culture, exhibiting God's option for the poor, is a theme with relatively few advocates in Britain today (but see Rowland and Vincent 1995).

The Lima Documents

The Lima documents on *Baptism, Eucharist and Ministry* (1982) and many responses to them have provided an international ecumenical touchstone for much of this new theology of Church. Essentially it calls the whole people of God to recognize that being Church is living in communion with God through Jesus in the Holy Spirit. The Church is called to proclaim and prefigure the Kingdom of God. To be a foretaste of the Kingdom in many different contexts, Christians are to be innovative in proclaiming good news in word and lifestyle. The Holy Spirit gives the community diverse, complementary gifts for service within the community itself and for communicating the gospel in healing, prayer, teaching and service.

The Lima texts recognize the varying models of Church and ministerial arrangements but consider a basic question appropriate to all:

> How, according to the will of God and under the guidance of the Holy Spirit is the life of the Church to be understood and ordered so that the Gospel may be spread and the community be built upon love?

We shall return in Chapters Three and Four to examine the theology of collaborative ministry but it must be touched on here primarily to show how the internal relatedness of the Church is not just a matter of convenience or of domestic interest only. We see today what scandal is caused by clergy overreaching the boundaries of their office, when the Pope acts autocratically, when a member of the hierarchy says that women are incapable of ordination because of their gender, or when laity are routinely treated as second-rate. The way the Church operates and inter-relates is no mere detail or irrelevance. It tells the world what it believes about all life and all relationships – whether it means to or not.

Regarding ordained ministry, Lima asserts that to fulfil its mission, the local church needs persons who are publicly and continually responsible for pointing to its fundamental depend-ence on Jesus Christ and therefore provide, through diversity of gifts, a focus of unity. This ministry of such persons is regarded as 'constitutive' for the life and work of the Church.

It argues that the Church has never been without persons holding specific authority and responsibility. Jesus chose and sent the disciples to be *witnesses* of the Kingdom (Matt. 10.1–8). The twelve were promised they would 'sit on thrones judging the twelve tribes of Israel' (Luke 22.30). A particular *role* was at-tributed to the twelve within the communities of the first gener-ation – they were *witnesses* to the Lord's life and resurrection (Acts 1:21–26). They led the community in prayer, teaching, breaking the bread, proclamation, and service (Acts 2.42–47; 6.2–6). The very existence of the twelve and other apostles dem-onstrates that from the beginning there were *differentiated roles within the community*. In other words, 'apostle' is a term cap-able of many meanings: herald, ambassador, leader, teacher, and pastor. The conclusion must be that, contrary to claims in the early twentieth century, it is not possible or appropriate to sug-gest that any particular form of ordained ministry may be said to have been instituted or willed specifically by Jesus Christ (Kerkhofs 1980).

All members of the believing community, ordained and lay together, are interrelated. On the one hand the Church needs ordained ministers to remind the community of the divine mis-sion in which they are engaged and of the grace of God on which they are dependent and by which they are built up. On the other hand, ordained ministry has no proper existence apart from, in one way or another, the local church community. Clergy cannot dispense with the recognition, support and encouragement of the communities to which they belong primarily *by baptism*.

Clodovis and Leonardo Boff

Base Community parishes in Third World countries have given churches in the West opportunities to reflect on the question, 'What is the Church?' Roman Catholic Bishops of Argentina in recent decades have committed their Church to the view that unlike the first evangelization of Latin America by missionaries, the new evangelization is to be the task of every baptized person as a live and active member of the Body of Christ. Against the prevailing forces of conservatism, small basic communities have moved away from a way of life centred on what the clergy are thinking and doing to one in which the participation of all is fostered in Eucharist, study, pastoral and teaching ministries, outreach, witness and evangelism. Some of the fruits of this way of being Church is that there is a new intimacy among the membership who share at great depth their lives together. They are learning to celebrate their faith liturgically and spontaneously and together to work for Kingdom values in society. The Puebla document encourages Church to be a place where race, gender, age, intelligence are all of no importance in comparison with the new commandment of the Lord for mutual love and the commitment to share in God's mission (Puebla 641).

Clodovis Boff (1981) has analysed the nature of Basic Christian Communities as characterized by evangelism – a sense of joy, hope, freedom, simplicity and welcome, community – sharing faith, prayer, Word, goods and problems, participatory and critical of Church and society attitudes, and militancy – committed in God's name to changing all that oppresses people and modelling a way of life inspired by God. As in the Church of every age the results are far from the ideal. The vital point here is that such communities place equal emphasis on their internal and external relationships. They are communities where belief is known and celebrated and where all are recognized as of equal value. But also they are committed to evangelism and to making a contribution to the health of society.

The Franciscan, Leonardo Boff stresses the role of the laity in Base Communities in contradiction to inherited patterns of Church based on hierarchy and institution rather than the dynamics of local community. Being the Catholic Church for Boff is not a matter of geography but of identity: the local church is not merely a piece of something larger or an insignificant outpost of a centralized institution (see Walton 1994). It is the place of *koinonia* where the Church springs from the people in many different forms and expressions (Boff 1986). Its primary intention is to proclaim the nearness of the Kingdom through the dynamics of Christian community as the 'praxis of liberation' (Walton 1994).

Jürgen Moltmann and J. B. Metz

Jürgen Moltmann (1981) has drawn out the significance of clergy and laity (without distinction) contributing to building up the local church as a mission station, where there is a concern for the poor and where the life of that community is in itself a working model of Kingdom values, a test case of its own gospel message. In a world of fragmented and frightened societies the *koinonia* spirit and practice of the local church offers a vital and critical witness through its potential for generating new patterns of redeemed relatedness and as experimental laboratories of public life and service (Mead 1994).

Moltmann insists that in the Church of God no one must be made to seem or feel inferior because all belong to a common people where no one should be deskilled or permanently marginalized. Similarly, J. B. Metz looks for a Church that is *of* people, not *for* people. He calls even the most affable clergy to stop doing things benignly for people as though acting for others out of their own strength. Instead they should develop their own maturity to be not only a leader but also truly a part of the community. Metz scorns the concept of the local church as a religious supermarket where people come, when they can, for religious ceremonies, but remain objects of a caring professional ministry. So we are challenged to work for a Church that is not providing a public service (like a post office or pub) but a communion of people sharing a common language, customs, and the memory of a common history. This community is not over against others who are not members or for security against those who are inferior, but a Church that can teach society a new meaning of the idea of 'the people' without the implication of adversarial tribalism.

Moltmann invites us constantly to revisit the ministry of Jesus. Does our Church retell the story of Jesus – combining human suffering and hopefulness with the story of Jesus? Unlike the scribes and pharisees, Jesus was renowned for being one *with* people. In the Kingdom of God, the subjects are brothers and sisters of Christ, not objects of the charity or even the mission of others (see Schüssler Fiorenza's 'discipleship of equals', 1984). Early missionaries like Paul discovered Christ *already present* in people and places, especially in 'the least of his brothers and sisters'. People who share resurrection life become subjects of their own history and *in Christ* take on a status of which no one can rob them. The impetus of the theology of the Church offered by Moltmann is towards a people who take the Church in their own hands through participation, solidarity, and working for common goals. At the heart of this Church lies the eucharistic celebration at which shared poverty makes everyone rich.

This new reformation aims at a way of being Church which goes beyond the institutional, in which its members are invited to grow up as the priesthood of all the baptized. Now it is possible to get excited by the prospect of becoming a Church in which people are not just taken care of (we all need this sometimes) but to see themselves as arising in all kinds of groups as a community of brothers and sisters (Gal. 3.28) where 'it shall not be so among you' (Matt. 20.26) and in which things are held in common (Acts 2.44). The other members of the Church are not self-selecting but given to us in all their variety by Jesus himself as partners in the struggle for maturity. Finally Moltmann asks us to be wary of becoming a confident congregation, turning into a congregationalist sect, a 'little flock' in the wrong sense, consciously élitist, a refuge for the fearful, rather than open to God and open to the world.

Christoph Schwöbel

Even more recently Christoph Schwöbel (1991), in describing 'the social shape of the Christian faith', describes Church as the place where Christian faith is the *content* of social relationships as an aid to the interpretation of the whole of reality and all personal experience. As a human organization, Church is a community of witness to God's revelation in Christ. It knows itself as formed by God's self-disclosure in Christ and as given the task of witnessing to this truth. Schwöbel describes the gospel as the truth about the destiny of the world. This is both the promise of final salvation and also the call to freedom. So the Church, as *the social form of the gospel*, holds the key to understanding all human life.

In particular, the sacraments of Baptism and Holy Communion together as the *practice* of the Church community reveal God's trinitarian action of creating (Father), reconciling (Son), and perfecting (Spirit), in turn giving shape to all human life, personally and socially. To *be Church*, for Schwöbel, is to be incorporated into God's life as part of his Covenant People, and so to have communion with Father, Son and Spirit. This action has the potential to reconstitute all life, offering the promise of forgiveness for the abuse of all human freedom. Such a way of being Church is impossible in isolation from the mainstream of human history. Rather it is living together hopefully, making a contribution, through God's grace, to holding the world together.

Conclusion

In their different ways, like lines of music creating a complex and joyful harmony, these texts and writers have, among many others, stimulated me to a vision of Church which can be both challenging and consoling. The test of authenticity is whether our working paradigm of Church helps us and all others to say a resounding 'Yes' to life in all its fullness, received as the overflowing blessing of the triune God. Laity and clergy, gathered and dispersed, can recognize their different and complementary parts in the task. The local church – formed by closeness to Jesus in the power of the Spirit – can continue to express the Father's love, helping to free society and creation from all that binds them. The practice of Christian community can be a white hot crucible of redemption for all.

3 ❧ CHURCH ROOTED IN THE TRINITARIAN GOD

Introduction

Another of the key elements of new hope in the ecumenical international theological conversation lies in the revision of our understanding of the nature of God and our relationship with God. It is becoming clearer that our relationship with the world and with God, rather than being thought of in static, unchanging terms, is better described as the interplay of mutual relationship. It is not enough to think of ourselves as merely other than God, but as intrinsically designed for communication with God, 'the receptacle of God's self-communication' (L. Boff 1988).

However, churches are usually distorted in their relating and manipulative in their dealings. Often churches are perceived as needy, rather than overflowing with Christ's love. An image that comes to mind is that of an industrial-sized vacuum cleaner. Churches, as we know all too well, can hoover up peoples' lives, money, time, spouses, and energy. Recently in a parish mission, the missioners visited door to door, asking people what the local church could do for them. People were truly amazed not to be asked to do something *for* the church. This vision of a hoover that blows, rather than sucks, is a long way from common practice. In reality many metaphors of the Church have to be held together, as indeed we find in the New Testament.

A Reconsideration of the Trinity

Churches across the world are rediscovering the truth that God is not one alone, and pondering again what we mean when we say 'Father, Son and Holy Spirit' – the Trinity. This theological development is in close harmony with renewed thinking about the nature of God's relationship with all creation and with human beings. After decades of theological deconstruction many are returning to trinitarian categories with a new confidence. This comes as a surprise to others. I remember after a talk I gave on rediscovering the Trinity, a devout lady commented kindly, 'Until you spoke, I'd never had any problems with the Trinity.'

For some church members the Trinity is simply integral to the biblical experience, to the Church's liturgy, and basic, orthodox Christianity, though its full import can be lost beneath repeated creeds and glorias. There always have been Christians who complain that the original faith of the early Church has been corrupted by doctrinal speculation. They often see the doctrine of the Trinity as an additional and unnecessary burden – a mathematical problem invented by those with too much time on their hands. Trinitarian theology is too ambitious for them – it borders on the edge of arrogance and presumption to make claims to knowledge of God's interior life. In partial answer I would be keen to accept that even when we have used up all our Christian language and concepts to speak of our experience of God, we have hardly begun. There must remain a healthy degree of mystery, held together with the wisdom of other faiths, and then *for everyone* a profound silence. Nevertheless we are inheritors of the biblical revelation and we have brains and tongues through which God enables us to continue – in the power of the Holy Spirit especially – to pursue the question of who God is. We have been promised by Jesus that the Spirit will continually lead us into all truth.

Although it must be wise to be cautious regarding any human claims to the knowledge of God, I take it as axiomatic that at the heart of all Christian theology lies the perennial question of what God must be like if he is to be at one and the same time true to his inner nature and yet also able to relate to humanity and be active in creation. The trinitarian doctrine is not an academic conundrum, but a way of articulating the experiences of Christians of being known by the God made known in Jesus through his Spirit. The fact that God is Trinity makes a world of difference to everything. As I summarized in *Transforming Priesthood* (1994):

First, God's being is most accurately understood by Christians as Trinity: a communion of Father, Son, and Holy Spirit. Second, it is essential to God's purpose for the universe that all relationships should be understood as echoing the trinitarian pattern. Third, the Church having a particular task to prepare the way for godly relationships in society and creation, must allow its ministerial arrangements to echo the trinitarian relationships of loving communion.

The wars, global tragedies and personal sufferings of humanity, made more widely known to more people this century, have been the crucible in which real theology can be done. In this context there has been less emphasis on the almightiness, transcendence, unmovability of God and more on his dynamic, relating and suffering aspects. The rediscovery of the reality of God as trinitarian is a direct product of this process in the modern world (Hill 1982).

A Brief History of Trinitarian Theology

It cannot be claimed that the New Testament contains a doctrine of the Trinity, as such. But we can trace there the development of hesitant experiments with phrases that express that the same God known in Abraham and the Jewish inheritance is also known in Jesus and the Spirit. The Father sends the Son, the Son shows the Father, the Spirit is with Jesus, Jesus sends the Spirit and 'I and the Father are one'. In the earliest worship of congregations around the Mediterranean, Christians knew themselves as in relationship with each other and with God through the Son and the Spirit. Today, hymns, intercessions, sermons, and meditations should always be trinitarian in character because the Church, even when it forgets or fails in its endeavours, has no other source than the love of God who is three in one.

The Council of Nicaea (AD 325) committed Christians to an understanding of God as being in relation. The Fathers of that Council defined that the Father and the Son shared the same substance. In his very being God is relational *communion*. The fourth-century Cappadocian theologians – Basil of Caesarea, Gregory of Nyssa, and Gregory of Nazianzus – continued the trinitarian work, particularly by emphasizing the place and work of the Holy Spirit. They too showed how *communion* lies at the heart of God's being. 'The substance of God, "God", has no ontological content, no true being, apart from communion' (Zizioulas 1985). The Cappadocian Fathers, against their Greek philosophical background, recognized that they were deliberately being innovative concerning a new and paradoxical conception of a united separation or a separated unity. They stressed that the persons of the Trinity owed deference to one another, rather than having a merely mathematical connection or relationship of subordination. The Cappadocians were offering a markedly new perception of the nature of God. The Father, Son and Spirit, as an inseparable *communion* of mutual love are nothing other than a single being. The trinitarian character is not added to the original single nature of God, but is all that God is. God is *communion*, a loving dynamism of three Persons in relation. To speak of Christ, therefore, always means referring at the same time to the Father and the Spirit.

The most characteristic word of the Cappadocians is *perichoresis*, meaning literally 'around a location', but used to speak of mutual indwelling, reciprocal deferring. The three Persons of the Trinity in perichoretic relationship do not simply take up an attitude of loving concern towards each other, but actually make each other who they are through loving relation. Their separate, different contribution to the trinitarian being and work is inseparable from the relationship between them (L. Boff 1988).

It follows, in the Cappadocian theology that 'person', as opposed to 'individual', becomes a concept only to be defined in terms of relation with others. In trinitarian terms, the loving relationship that is God is an overflowing, available movement, communicating in the processes of creation and redemption (Gunton, in Schwöbel 1991).

Trinitarian theology was not developed significantly in the Middle Ages nor, indeed, up to the mid twentieth century and certainly has not been brought into serious engagement with our thinking about the nature of the Church. Instead, we took authority models for the Church's inner communications from the dying embers of the Roman Empire and the trappings of mediaeval monarchy. If the Church's personal relationships and distribution of power were to dare to be an echo of the trinitarian being of God, it would have the potential to commend its own interior life as a pattern for all human relating – a practice rooted in the creator and saviour God. A triune God whose inner life may be expressed in terms of mutual indwelling, implies a

Church in which there are no permanent structures of subordination but rather, overlapping patterns of mutual relationship. The same person or group of persons will be sometimes subordinate and at other times superordinate, according to the gifts and graces being exercised depending on need.

Implications for the Church's Life

The Church has, therefore, through communion with the Trinity, the responsibility and the ability to make a distinctive contribution to current questions regarding the proper ordering of personal relations in society generally and relations between the human race and its global environment. The New Testament indicates that God sees the destiny of humanity as bound up with that of the entire cosmos. The Church exists to help humanity share in God's mission. If God's great project is that the whole cosmos should come to maturity, the triune character of 'God-self' should be witnessed in the Church's life. Here Paul's concept of Church as *koinonia*, communion or community is reflected in God's own life. The Church is called in Christ and through the Spirit, to model or to be a sign of that *communion* which is the very being of God and the shape of his desire for the perfection of the cosmos. God's intention that creation and humanity should have at their heart the power and the will for mutual interrelatedness becomes the internal shape and the external witness and gospel of the Church.

At a time when many are questioning the twentieth-century culture of individualism when societies are in adversarial inner conflict; when the struggle to accept rather than avoid a multi-faith and multi-culture society is pressing; the Church faces many challenges. Can Christians find the courage and wisdom to discern what of present culture is creative and what is better rejected? A trinitarian faith – far from being a handicap – is probably the most potent and sophisticated means to engaging in dialogue with society. At a time when mechanistic approaches to creation, science, human relationships and the work environment are all under fire, a Church which itself models the trinitarian divine life could be the midwife of the holistic life for which many are longing.

The Church has a vision of how the Trinity opens up a concept of being human, reversing the so-called truth of secular science that human beings in relation are merely one plus one plus one. As an alternative to this artificial view of human relations, we may propose an understanding based on the work of an artist. The idea of the painting does not come first, followed by the work of painting. Rather there is a dynamic relationship between artist, situation, chosen materials and observer, and in the midst of this process the idea is conceived and conveyed.

Before moving on to make specific proposals for how we might begin to understand the role of the priest who will oversee the local church's development – a vital role indeed – we need to make a short digression to examine our understanding of the Church (ecclesiology) taking an eschatological trinitarianism as the key. How would it be if we used the traditional four marks of the Church – unity, holiness, catholicy and apostolicy – rooted in a relational approach to the nature of all reality?

Unity

The origins of the earliest Christian communities are not as clear to us as was assumed earlier in the twentieth century. Whatever their relationship with Jesus' own intention, at the heart of the New Testament understanding of Church lies the recurring concept of *koinonia*. This points to three vital aspects of Church: connectedness with God, with other members of the Christian community, and with the world. Working towards all three in simultaneous relation is a vision we can constantly set before ourselves, hard as it is to keep them in balance. Just as we believe the persons of the Trinity to constitute each other through relatedness, the icon of harmonious difference, worshippers in the Church by grace and discipline may hope to grow into communion with the Trinity. In the reading and interpretation of the Word and sharing of bread and wine, especially, Anglicans believe that Christ through the Spirit grants communion with himself in community with all others who are through Christian community both sharing in the life of the Trinity and attempting to make the eschatological future a present reality. Such unity is not dependent on doctrinal agreement but allows of diversity in knowing the mystery of God and giving expression to that partial knowledge.

So unity, once rooted in the security of conforming to an orthodox pattern of ordained ministry, has a more promising beginning in the act of baptism, the keystone for understanding the Christian experience of *communion*. Baptism has four inter-locking themes:

- It is intimately connected with the death and resurrection of Jesus Christ.
- It grants incorporation into the life of God and the Christian community.
- It is a commissioning, in company with all other baptized people, for working for the fulfilment of God's mission.
- It is specifically the acceptance of the trinitarian invitation to work here and now for the coming Kingdom – inaugurated eschatology.

Participation in the Eucharist enables the baptizing commun-ity to be deepened in its exposure to God's blessing and ability to risk sharing responsibility for the future destiny of humanity. In constantly recalling the Lord's death until he comes, the Christian community receives God's blessing to continue Jesus' project of bringing creation to fulfilment.

Part of the current battle for the character of Anglicanism centres on the question of what kind of unity? The temptation when Churches feel threatened and when traditional resources are scarce, is to move towards a gathered Church of the like-minded, who in blunt terms are willing to pay for an inward-looking, monochrome Church with which they can agree in almost every respect and will work hard for its growth. The de-velopment of this kind of community, where members travel through several other parishes to be part of the local church of their choice is now a recognized feature of a pluralist society. In human terms we can recognize how varied are the operational theologies of local churches – and how much this is governed by the present minister in charge. It is equally clear that in the long run this approach presents a threat to the vision of providing a church for the entire community – frustrating as this can be most of the time.

Given that an eschatological-trinitarian ecclesiology regards the Church as called primarily to be a sign of reconciliation to the world – made possible only through the costly and non-manipulative love of God in Christ on the cross – we need a vision of a complex, untidy, comprehensiveness which in humility defers to many spiritualities and insights into God's being. Such a rainbow effect of theologies and practices held in tension resounds best with the New Testament and much of the best of the lay catholic Christian tradition. Paul affirmed the great gifts of the Spirit but discouraged a sense of competition or denial of the gifts of others. If in doubt, the higher way is that of vulnerable love (1 Cor. 13). To work out what it is to be in the world, but not of it, is to take with utter seriousness and often genuine enjoyment the particular context in which a local church is set. Whose culture does Christ's Church dare to disown? So often, without emotional or intellectual rigour, in the name of the gospel we fail to see the divine in popular cultures and limit the Church by a 'haute-cuisine' aesthetic (Mouw 1994).

Community, civic, and political life have such a desperate need to be in dialogue with the values of the trinitarian gospel. This is part of the mission of the local church – though not from the loftiness of having ready answers, but in risky and often controversial dialogue and through the witness of sacrificial practice. What point is there in the congregation in church singing about the seat of judgement unless in the real world church people are prepared to wrestle with the practical problems of justice and equity?

In summary: the unity of the local church, rooted in trinitarian *communion,* means this. As communion with God, fellowship in Christian community and as the proclamation of communication of the present working out of God's final peace, the local church both receives the gift of reconciled difference and works for its completion among all people. Every temptation should be avoided to settle for a unity with God, with fellow Christians and with society that fails to take account of the actual complexity or fails to embrace creation as a whole.

Holiness

The Church has a vocation to be a community of holiness, which is not the same as being self-righteous. Rather it is about being a community in which faith, hope and love are habitual. This community life should aim to offer the same attractive picture of God as that presented by the New Testament. In a trinitarian ecclesiology we can describe holiness as the practice of being radiant with the patterns of mutual deference and courtesy that characterize the community of Godself. Instead of a social gospel of morality, the local church in word and deed, after the pattern of Jesus, points to a way of being that mirrors the divine life.

This vision is more than just idle hope, because it has been made possible in the costly action on Golgotha. Despite tragic failures in the past, by attending to its own inner life, as a partial revelation of the holiness of God, the Church is called to work towards its task of being a foretaste of what all life will be when God's will is accomplished. Every detail of bureaucracy, of employment, of dealing in the business world, or offering pastoral care should aim to be, in embryo, an illustration of the destiny of all creation. Church history is full of reminders of Christian lapses into replacing love and peace with dominance and legal codes, but this must not deter us from having a vision which is always elusive but never, by the grace of God, mere fantasy.

The trinitarian operation of the Church's unity as communion, community and communication bears the hallmark of the gift and invitation of God who in the relatedness of his being is the source of blessedness.

Catholicity

The Church is catholic in that its membership is open to all, in that only through interrelatedness with others can a particular eucharistic assembly call itself 'Church', and in that its interior life is never separate from its shared concern for the wholeness of creation. This means the Church must always be challenged when it excludes people from membership on grounds of doctrine, gender, ethics, culture or race. It is not pedigree but Christ-like qualities that make for the catholic Church.

There are natural fears that so much emphasis on the local church will be at the expense of the catholic. However, in discussion in many places I have discovered an unwillingness to make a satisfactory differentiation between the local and the universal. For example there are victim-like church members who will blame the bishop, the diocese, or the Church of England for their misfortunes. It is true that we need to be vigilant for repressiveness in churches that diminish humanness in patterns of violence or claims to unlimited sovereignty (Thiselton 1995). Churches, like any organization, need to be suspected for their tendency to ignore local variation and need, and to perpetuate patterns of injustice. A proper vulnerability in bishops, archdeacons and diocesan officers could allow for a more honest exchange over institutional issues. But it is a reality to be faced that there are clergy who, choosing to ignore recent theological insights about the universal Church being found in every particular or local church, are holding back the proper development of a new model of Church by continuing to espouse understandings of priesthood that are no longer appropriate.

This is because the most truthful theology recognizes that it is the local church as a body that comes before consideration of particular ministries. Certainly local churches need the wisdom of itinerant apostolic clergy who bring new breadth to the local scene; but once resident in the local church those clergy should see themselves, as far as is possible, as one with the local community, rather than semi-detached even though, as we shall see later, that is not the whole story. The reality is, of course, that one day they will move elsewhere, but for the time being, God, the local community and the bishop are asking that priest to exercise a ministry *of* and *within* the local church.

To return to the nature of the catholicity of the whole Church, a renewed emphasis on the humanity of Christ in all its vulnerability, together with a sense of openness to the Spirit will be more in tune with a Church anticipating in small and provisional ways the final purposes of God. Also, claims to catholicity should not be substantiated in terms of clerical pedigrees, the restrictive practices of institutions or in a spirit of confessional rivalry. No local church *should* presume to claim to possess 'catholicity' because of the orthodoxy of its belief or practice. Yet we continue to do so. Catholicity is recognizing that only in dialogue and relationship with other communities of Jesus Christ can the truth in Christ be known and celebrated. A local church that is not catholic in this way is not a local church.

Apostolicity

To be apostolic used to be a test of whether an unbroken mechanical link could be proved down the centuries between ordained clergy and the twelve apostles. A more accurate understanding in the light of present theological discourse is that, as catholicity is the whole local church community in relation in geographical world terms, apostolicity is to be in relation *through time*. The local church will be relating with the churches down the centuries that have witnessed to the life, death and resurrection of Jesus and also will be making connections *now* with the eschatological desire of God:

> The church manifests [apostolic] order and succession when its behaviour imitates the Lord's when its teaching is faithful to the apostles' message and when its leaders are trusted exemplars worthy of imitation by all. (Mitchell 1982)

The sharing of the many to become one people of God who share in trinitarian communion in the Eucharist and offer to the world a diagram of the Kingdom is a clear sign of the apostolic Church. As such it needs no protection, dogmatism or strategies of domination. In vulnerability learned from Christ it is known for its ability and willingness to be companions with the weak and marginalized in society.

In summary, apostolicity refers to the Church's intimate connectedness with its past and its future. As the sign and foretaste of God's peace it is constituted both by its roots in the events of Jesus' ministry and the rise of the witnessing community and also in the eschatological wholeness of the Christ in whose hands the Father has placed the world's final destiny.

Trinitarian Relationships Proclaim the Gospel

A local church should be able to show how we are identified by virtue of our membership of one another. We are essentially community and without each other we become less than human. We know that by temperament some of us more readily find our energy alone, rather than in company, but whether we are naturally extrovert or introvert, to be human is to be in relation in one way or another. Recent findings on personal break-down suggested that those who find themselves in deepest trouble or on the edges of the law and effective everyday life will usually have fewer than ten people who care and with whom they are in relationship. One of the urgent needs of so many people in Britain today is for structures that build up social coherence rather than reinforce isolation, competition for resources and disintegration. In this sense the model of Church proposed here is highly subversive. The William Temple principle that churches exist for the sake of non-members should encourage the vision of the local church as perhaps offering that life-line of social relationships that otherwise would be unavailable to someone. Without sociality we become inhuman. It is a built-in condition of being human to enter, to some degree at least, into reciprocal relationship with others who may be very different from ourselves.

In a society that thrives on adversarial competition and the assumption that a few winners will mean a majority of losers, proclaiming the gospel is overdue. Given the vision of God's Kingdom, already established as a reality by God's work in Jesus Christ, Christians are called to create fertile conditions in which human relations may be transformed here and now in concreteness. The Church is here to untie the distorted networks of communication between humanity and creation and to replace them with ways of relating rooted in the trinitarian image. It is a Christian doctrine that to be a human person is to acknowledge and rejoice in the truth that we make each other who we are. To be human in the Christian sense of that word is to intend the growth and fullness of another and at the same time to be so-intended by them. To be open to the Trinity is at the same time to be open to all humanity and to creation. It is as if there is a watermark set within humanity and all the cosmos which portrays the overflowing and interdependent life and loving relationship we call 'God'.

Evangelism therefore is not the duty of drawing more people into churches so that they may be full and prosperous. Rather, evangelism is the patient and courteous listening and conversation with those who are struggling to grow up. It is the invitation to say 'yes' to joining the mission of God – to travelling hopefully to new and unexplored places in the company of those who want to be part of God's coming Kingdom, that *shalom* which characterizes God's final intention for all. This is not the innocent optimism of the 1970s and 1980s, but the knowing, subversive, and often costly creation of a community – focused on the cross of Christ – that works for God's good End (Warren 1994).

A Church that Shares in God's own Agenda

Faith is to recognize and respond to the presence of that God who invites all humanity to relationship with one another, with creation and with Father, Son, and Spirit. Human sin lies in denying this truth and refusing to make those connections. The work of Christ on the cross is to restore these fragmented relationships. This redemption is truly 'a ransom for many' as the Son's taking flesh, proclaiming the Kingdom, dying and rising really does effect the renewing, reordering and redirecting of creation towards God's final intention. 'In the light of the theology of the Trinity everything looks different' (Gunton 1991).

So often our society and even church members have a way of speaking of God and Jesus as though important religious experience is all located in the past and only the recalling of its memory offers inspiration for today. The trinitarian God is not remote and lofty but engages deeply in the heart of all life. Equally we must resist the present tendency to locate God's activity entirely in the present and in only one location, deliberately rejecting the witness of the past or the rest of the world. We need Goethe's reminder that 'He who cannot draw on three thousand years is living from hand to mouth'.

As we have seen already, one of the truly exciting developments of much recent theological thought is known as 'eschatological' because it deals with the past and the present in the light of God's final future desire for all creation. There is a major biblical imperative to read back God's invitation to those who wish to work with him from the future in which he promises that all things will be brought to final maturity in Christ (Zizioulas 1985).

We know from the prophets, the Psalms, Jesus' preaching and life, and the agenda of early Christian communities, the shape of God's desire for creation and humanity is to be recognized in reciprocal respect and justice (Boff 1988, Moltmann 1989). Essentially what is involved is a recognition that God is at work in past, present and future, inviting us, not to see history as merely a succession of events but as a dynamic relationship.

Deciding How to be Church Here and Now

One way to explain how any local church might face the regular task of deciding how to be Church here and now is to consider the metaphor of a quadrant, or perhaps better a compass. At the centre the local church – the living body of Christ in reality – enquires how to be obedient to God's will here and now.

There are four main pointers to this ecclesiological compass – how we know which way God is directing the Church.

(1) The first is the Jesus event – the incarnational ministry and proclamation of the Kingdom followed through to death on the cross and ratified by God's raising him from death. The witness to this event in the church of biblical times and in the centuries until now provides a significant direction finder for the Church that seeks to serve God's mission. All too often, though, this glorious and sometimes inglorious past has been taken as the only pointer. For example, many who oppose women's ordination cannot understand how something not contained in the Christian past can be possible in the present. This is to forget that tradition is a progressing and developing memory of God's work in Jesus as well as a genetic coding for the present and future.

(2) Second, there is the presence of the Paraclete. We were promised by Jesus that those who wish to obey God can rely on the ever-present Holy Spirit, leading into all truth. What was true for Jesus at his baptism at the hands of John – to be one of the poor and the marginalized and as

such one of God's own children, choosing God as Father and therefore God's passionate desire for his world – can also be true for us. Together, under the Spirit, God's new covenant people are empowered, taught how to love, directed, upheld and given wisdom. They are shown by the Spirit how to temper Canon Law and how to bear with one another in their different woundedness. So often in the Book of Revelation we read 'Listen to what the Spirit is saying'. Being led into the truth is a continuing and often painful saga which goes beyond the limits of past traditions, allows churches to do things for the very first time, gives freedom for the Christian life to be sometimes a party, always discerning into the heart of things, and never complete.

(3) The third pointer represents context: who we are here in this particular place, what people we are among, what are the crying needs and pains wherever the universal Church is locally present. Theology and mission do not stride along Olympian heights, commissioned by a timeless and lonely God, speaking formal and repeatable oracles. In fear and trembling, humility and vulnerability Christ's Church needs the confidence to listen attentively. Disconcertingly to recognize context is to know that attitudes change with experience and certain hardfast opinions get dislodged in new circumstances – consider the ways in which many of us have had our views of the place of women (in general and in the church) altered through experience. The context of the local church is also – together with revelation and the Spirit – primary data for tuning its message and witness of reconciliation. The gospel is not declaimed ever the same on tablets of stone, but will sound very different on different occasions with differing peoples (Donovan 1982, Warren 1995). So, Scripture, Spirit and context *together* form the agenda of the local church.

(4) The last pointer represents God's desire for the fulfilment of all things in Christ. The mirror image of celebrating the Lord's death until he comes – in the Eucharist – is to be a Church that anticipates that End. It is to be a Christian

community of brothers and sisters, reaching out into the world in such a way as to be a sign of what is to come – a foretaste of the loving interrelationships and dying in order to live that characterizes heaven. It is to practise being the first shoots, the first blossom on the bough which show that summer is coming. On its own this would be too great a burden to bear, but in the company of the other three pointers – our knowledge of the often fragmented New Testament churches, of the consoling and energizing presence of the Spirit, and of the freedom to experiment according to our circumstances – we can enjoy being drawn into becoming already something of what we know God has in store for us (Rev. 7.15–17).

All these four interrelated points of the ecclesiological compass of the church that is the 'background radiation of the resurrection' (Polkinghorne 1994) as well as the firstfruits of the Kingdom to come, interrelate to form a cross at the heart of the universe, like some dynamic interrelating scientific symbol. Revelation and Eschaton, Spirit and context cannot in the end be separated.

To summarize: the Church's agenda is to be embraced as a four-dimensional open quest. It involves making connections in any one time and place between:

- the inherited tradition of 2,000 years of Christian experience triggered by the life, death and resurrection of Jesus Christ
- the promised presence of the Holy Spirit leading to the truth
- the kaleidoscope of contemporary contexts
- and the invitation to live in and work for, even now, God's passionate desire for the fulfilment of the whole creation.

4 ⚜ EQUAL AND DIFFERENT MINISTRIES

A chief focus for this book arises from the reality that the Church of England over the next quarter-century will look very different from in the immediate past. Instead of stipendiary male clergy being the mainstay of pastoral activity in relatively small territories, the future will probably bring teams of male and female Christian ministers working in collaboration over quite wide areas in the countryside and across several former parishes in urban centres. There are many factors at work, including the painful anxiety of those who would prefer nothing to change.

Throughout this book a cumulative set of premises have built up. These include the primary data that

- A local church is nothing more or less than a mission station.
- To be Church is to be a collection of people in ministry with a missionary agenda.

This is not to say that most of these ministries will be church-focused. Of course the church exists in dispersion, wherever its members find themselves during the week when they are not meeting for worship or to make plans and be encouraged for the work of sharing God's mission. The reality is that most Christians are properly at the tasks of parenting, earning a living if they can find a job, collaborating with others in the neighbourhood, engaging in care for others, or witnessing to Christ in word and deed. Only a tiny minority – except in very small churches – will be required to minister to the ministers, to focus the mission of the whole community.

The new way of being Church will have to take for granted reduced numbers of stipendiary clergy and will not be able financially to maintain the old infrastructures. Positively it will increasingly be made up of people who are naturally inclined to want a full and mature place in any human organization of which they are a member, and who own and celebrate a rich inheritance of New Testament theology which, as we shall see, expects coresponsible sharing. Any form of leadership ministry, therefore, whether by a single person or a team of some kind, will never be thought of as a substitute for the ministry of anyone else. Rather it will be seen as a focus for making sure that everyone knows and is supported and chastened in their own ministries.

Ministry and Church Cannot be Separately Defined

Gradually I have built up a vision of 'an eschatological-trinitarian ecclesiology' – a way of being Church that begins now to show what the End will be, according to the unity in difference of the community that God is. Also we have seen how ministries can only truly be described and lived out in close relationship to the whole Church.

The logic of this approach was to begin by readdressing the question of God – not only what he has done for us, but what he has shown us of his inner being and purpose. We have seen how his mission is to bring to fruition in kaleidoscopic patterns of unity the End of creation so as to echo his own trinitarian life of *perichoresis* – of interrelationship and mutual deference. Only in these terms do we have adequate tools to understand what kind of Church is required – not in itself – but to be the firstfruits of that destiny of love.

Principles of Collaborative Ministry

A picture that comes to mind of traditional church ministry is of a solitary clerical figure straining every muscle to push a wheel-barrowful of bricks up a very steep hill. If the vicar manages to get near the top of this hill he is thought well of and is rewarded by the muted background applause of a cricket match.

A further stage of development has been the possibility of laity sometimes being included as 'helpers' of the busy clergy, so as to free the vicar for his real and important task. Helping the vicar is not collaborative ministry nor is it the bringing to birth of a new model of Church. The empowerment of the whole body of Christ in ministries lies at the heart of a coresponsible church:

The fundamental role of the leader is to make collegiality

possible. The role of the one in charge is not that of making a 'personal' decision after taking the advice of others into account. For in that case it would still be 'his' decision. His role is rather to make it possible, in so far as it depends upon him, for there to be a common decision which commits each member to the decision . . . A true leader will find his place when he has succeeded in helping the others to find theirs. (Suenens 1968)

If only more lay leaders, Readers, clergy and bishops could truly hear and live by this insight! Instead we take upon ourselves responsibilities which are not ours alone and we reap the reward we deserve in being put on a pedestal only shortly to be knocked down again. Ministry is not a solo activity. As women explore priesthood for themselves they are offering the whole church opportunities to ask, 'What is our model of authority?'

The End of Scapegoating

There has been a TV advert for an international company in which, despite the best endeavours of the roving reporter to give credit for achievements to a single individual, the worldwide team insisted that they had 'done it together'. When it comes to laying blame for lack of vitality or outright failure, churches do more than their fair share. 'If only we had a different vicar in this parish . . . ' 'If only the laity were not so . . .' 'If only someone took notice of me . . .' 'No one else will do anything here but me . . .' The Church has its victims by the score, and the wasting sickness of blaming others constantly debilitates our energy and hope. If we're in the business of exchanging clichés, how about 'The trouble with the clergy is we've only the laity to choose them from' or 'If ever you find that perfect church, for heaven's sake don't join it or you'll ruin it'.

More seriously, we need to hear warnings both of David Jenkins and of Dietrich Bonhoeffer if we presume to raise a prophetic voice. The former once said in a lecture that if we find the taste for prophecy growing in us, we had better give it up for our own sake. The true Old Testament prophets spoke *unwillingly*, when driven to it by a God who chooses surprising people for his tasks, and prepared for it by quite ordinary lives centred on meditation and praise. Bonhoeffer insists that God hates visionary dreaming. It is so easy for any of us to set ourselves up over against the community that has nourished us and make criticisms that imply that Christian community is of our own making. 'When his ideal picture is destroyed, he sees the community going to smash. So he becomes, first an accuser of his brethren, then an accuser of God, and finally the despairing accuser of himself' (Bonhoeffer 1949, 1992). René Girard's writings in the field of anthropology have examined in depth the mechanism of scapegoating in human society. He argues that Jesus was God's message to humanity to put an end to a religious practice rooted in violence once and for all. After the crucifixion of Jesus outside the city wall as the ultimate human scapegoat, Girard suggests his disciples should be finding every way possible to stop reacting to difficult situations by apportioning blame, not least by practising mature interdependency. Church history is sadly filled with evidence of a refusal to hear this message and distorted by the conception of God as exacting the death of Jesus as a sacrifice for sin. (See Girard 1986 and 1987.)

The theology of mission and ministry that undergirds the development of Local Ministry is rooted in three principles which move beyond adversarial and dualistic relatedness towards deep mutual respect:

1. The first is a renewed understanding of baptism, supported by respected scholars of all the major denominations, and experienced as authentic in the lives of many Christians. This emphasizes that every committed member has a rightful share in the mission and ministry of the body of Christ.

2. The second principle arises from a vision of collaborative ministry in which local churches regard themselves as corporate agents of mission, increasingly deploying local people in positions of leadership, and some would add, including where appropriate, ordination.

3. The third principle is a view of the clergy, in both urban and rural areas, no longer as isolated and omnicompetent ministers, but as those who evoke and support collaborative Local Ministry Teams of many kinds. These

principles lead to a radical revision of the shape of the ministry offered in, and by, the local church. Specifically, they lead to five developments:

1. Laity who are aware of themselves as the *subject*, rather than simply the *object*, of ministry. That is, to an acceptance of the responsibility of the whole people of God as the primary agents of Christian ministry, rather than being a group of people who are merely the recipients of ministry.

2. A body of clergy who act collegially rather than in isolation from the gifts of the laity and of other clergy.

3. Opportunities being developed for laity together with Readers and clergy to engage in the whole spectrum of the church's mission. This would include church-focused ministries, but for the vast majority of laity it would be a recognition that the main focus of their ministry lies in the opportunities presented by their everyday responsibilities and challenges amongst the people and in the communities with whom they are engaged.

4. The realization that groupings wider than a single parish, such as increasingly large benefices, deaneries, local ecumenical projects or locally negotiated groupings are likely to be the operative agents of the local church of the future.

5. The recognition of the implications for training and educating clergy and laity, both initially and on a continuing basis, and for the supportive roles of diocesan officers.

The developments in understanding the nature of Church in Roman Catholic contexts since the Second Vatican Council have contributed to the international ecumenical understanding (as witnessed also in the documents of Puebla, Lima and Porvoo). Roman Catholics have led the way in realizing that the full impact of Vatican II lies in a shift from a hierarchical institutional model to a community people-of-God model. James Coriden, for example, has argued that just as the Church is essentially collegial in structure, so also is ministry (Coriden 1977).

Team ministry, so often associated – and not always favourably – with the ordained, is in fact the logic for all Christian ministry.

In a coresponsible church, opportunities will be found to show that laity are not helpers of the clergy but are to be recognized as empowered through the Holy Trinity to witness to the resurrection and bring forward the Kingdom of God. Every baptized person has a share in the talents and convictions of the Spirit (1 Cor. 12.7) and serves through the gifts of Christ himself: 'I do not call you servants, I call you friends', Jesus says to the apostles. The friend does not ask how he must help but actually enters into the cause of his friend and 'owns' it. All recognize the call to holiness and to growth in human maturity. Clergy and laity are not distinct in this matter. *(See Lumen Gentium 40 and 44.)*

Laity are not there to *help* the priest because he is so busy or has so many parishes. Nor are the laity there to provide administration while the clergy go about God's 'higher' business. What minefields there are for parish and diocese when a dichotomy opens up between routine maintenance and mission, between administration and mission, finance and training or between the holy and the profane.

There has been much in the past twenty-five years of ecumenical theologizing about how to be Church that gives encouragement – we are living through a time of transition. In our present church structures we still look to highly trained priests, who automatically belong to a separate class of people, either from their own or the church members' (conscious or unconscious) choice. The new minister is taken aback and rendered helpless when the churchwarden says, 'In this parish we put our clergy on a pedestal – and there's nothing you can do about that!' Hopes of a new way of being Church will be hampered by immature dependency on leaders defined by class, prestige, and élitism, until we are educated out of this frame of mind and freed to find our security in a spirituality of vulnerability.

Letting go of Hierarchy

Now that it is established that ordained ministry should never be conceived of apart from the church that is all that is locally visible of the One, Holy, Catholic and Apostolic Church, we can say that, essentially, the priest is one of the community of disciples of Jesus Christ. Some readers will wish to take exception to the term 'priest'. Its origins and history certainly do make it a problematic term, but generally within Anglican circles it looks as if it is here for some time yet. I see no strong suggestion of an alternative term like 'presbyter' finding general acceptance. 'Minister' as a general term does seem to find more favour than at one time, but to be pragmatic in this book, I shall speak of the minister in charge of a local church (whether a single parish or a considerably larger territory) as 'the parish priest'. At a time of great change and flexibility some securities are required; transition is not about detaching completely from what has gone before.

The ministry team with the presiding priest are all primarily members of the missionary community that is the local church. With their fellow Christians they are called to share in bringing about the wholeness and reconciliation that God wills now and in the future. On the trinitarian principle of *perichoresis* (which is code for a community of difference and mutual deference), everyone is recognized as a minister, commissioned by their baptism. The parish priest has the particular task of being a distributing focus for the ministry team and the whole Church. It remains one of the unresolved problems of the Church how simultaneously to affirm the ministry of the rank and file of the local church and at the same time recognize the specifically essential work of the priest.

One of the pressure points in the debate is increasingly related to payment. If one is paid to be a Christian minister, what difference does that make? Does it necessarily have to diminish those who are unpaid or part-paid? In society generally status is given by high salaries. But there is doubt that clergy receive a payment related to performance or seniority. The majority of clergy receive the same basic pay, which is better called a stipend – a living allowance. As the Church's financial problems increase as inevitably they will in the foreseeable future, the proportion of local church ministries rewarded financially is sure to decline. If the connection becomes ever closer between the giving of the local community and the priest there will be pressure for clergy to listen much more to the desires of the whole Church. In some ways this may be fruitful and to be applauded. But the role of the priest is also partly detached and prophetic. It would be disastrous if the overwhelming mood of the local church were to drive towards an inward-looking congregationalism with some agenda which was not recognizably Christian. The question lurks stubbornly, how many people are willing to pay for what kind of Church? The training of the clergy, the synodical processes, preaching and local church decisions are all grist to the mill of 'whither ecclesiology'? The identity of Anglicanism cannot be left to chance – will the future be driven by an honest dialogue between what is essential and what is possible here and now? Who decides the answer to such questions? What do we mean by leadership in this context?

In an eschatological-trinitarian ecclesiology clergy and laity enhance one another. Uniqueness-in-relationship potentially avoids old arguments about clerical superiority and collusions about exclusive priestly spirituality. There is, of course, a sense in which anyone who has the potential giftedness to fulfil a role, once appointed to it will grow through grace and experience deeper and deeper into that role. This is true of churchwardens, youth leaders, teachers of the faith, those who offer a ministry of welcome, not to mention clergy and bishops. Each must always be careful to observe the John the Baptist principle, 'He must increase while I decrease', to ensure that trinitarian relations are being pursued. This is the kind of vulnerable authority for all to exercise, rather than depending on formal legitimation and institutional status.

In summary, each member of the Church, whatever their particular ministry, is at heart a disciple of Jesus Christ. Clergy have no existence except in relationship with fellow members of the baptized community; their own unique contribution is created and sustained within relationships of mutuality with their fellow ordained ministers, just as the persons of the Trinity exist in relationship:

> Gregory of Nazienzen shows how the Son has everything in common with the Father and the Spirit except being Father or Spirit, and the Spirit possesses everything the Father and Son possess except being Father or Son. (Zizioulas 1985)

In a trinitarian Church order is not imposed by one all-powerful force. In an eschatologically ordered Church, hope and salvation for all are intrinsic to the agenda. Any Church which introduces permanent states of above and below, important and not important, in its membership has not understood the significance of the mystery of the Trinity.

I take it that a relational view of ministry outflanks previous arguments as to whether or not the priest possesses an indelible character or whether ordination is about function or being. All ministry is that of Christ himself, who is himself permanently in relationship with the Father and the Spirit. The ordained minister is nothing in himself or herself, apart from the community and possesses nothing for himself or herself alone. The priest certainly does not provide a church for the laity to belong to. The collaborative ministries of the whole Church provide the vehicle by which the reconciling and costly work of Christ, in and through the Father and the Spirit, is made available to the world.

A Positive View of the Place of Readers

Readers have been consistently referred to throughout the book so far, but at this point I want to register how vital a role the future could hold for them. At first sight, for some Readers Local Ministry could seem to be a threat. Here are devoted laity who have given time and energy to becoming trained for a Reader ministry which is concerned with liturgy, preaching and teaching but always in a pastoral context. *Faith in the Countryside* describes the tradition of Readers as usually being visible only in the absence of clergy, taking services of Morning or Evening Prayer. Conversations with Readers reveal how they have often felt underused and rather at the mercy of their relationship with the vicar of the parish – 'a gap-filling dogsbody' (Archbishop's Commission on Rural Areas 1990). The fact that this Report has so little to say positively about Reader ministry speaks volumes. However, as with all ministry, that of Readers must constantly be reviewed and, if necessary, be reconceived (Hiscox 1991).

There has been an argument that all Readers should be ordained deacon, presumably implying that the Church of England should have a permanent diaconate. This seems a very unlikely possibility not least because, apart from being a probationary year for priests, the Church – and here I mean the vast majority of worshippers – can discern so little difference in deacons except in what they may not yet do liturgically. It has been suggested – if the Church would invest in a permanent diaconate – that instead of an untidy involvement of laity in public reading, administering communion, visiting the sick, leading house groups and so on, that such roles should be filled by Readers made deacon. This might be commended in the cause of consistency but in my view it would rob the *laity* of their hardly realized sense of sharing in the Church's authority to be the body of Christ. Most Readers are proud to be lay. Ministry belongs to the whole people of God as a gift and any attempt to suggest that public ministry is always the prerogative of the ordained, flowing in the direction of the laity as objects, should be resisted.

For many Readers it is precisely their lay status that is so important. Readers as a distinctive group are highly qualified with training that can often be equally, if not more rigorous than that offered to some of the clergy. This can sometimes represent a threat to clerical authority, requiring everyone to recall that God has given to his Church a richly variegated variety through the work of the Holy Spirit (Carey and Hind 1978). Readers should be regarded as a vital theological resource especially for teaching and preaching. The Reader has the bishop's licence and in practical terms has a stronger claim to being part of the structures. Certainly members of Local Ministry Teams will not all usually be invited to preach – simply because of their membership of the team – unless this important ministry is to be devalued.

When Local Ministry becomes a key to mission and ministry in the parishes Readers will always be part of any team that is created. No ministry exists properly by itself. Just as in the case of the parish priest, they will be able to show solidarity with laity on such teams by entering fully into the processes that make a team come into existence and maintain its life. Similarly when there is training taking place, Readers will hopefully not take the view, 'I've done all this before', but recognize how in team learning they have a great contribution to make from their accumulated experience, biblical knowledge, common sense, and loving concern for the development of other, newer ministries. Readers, with their commitment to lay education are in a position to place more emphasis on their own commitment to Continuing Ministerial Education now that it is more widely available. There is plenty of recent evidence that where Readers are taken seriously and treated with sensitivity, many are already playing a vital role as invaluable lay members of teams. They can be a stabilizing and supportive influence, especially in contributing experience and the deeper background study demanded by their training.

It has not been possible in the past for all Readers to share in Continuing Ministerial Education (CME). The Church now urgently requires all in positions of leadership to be frequently renewing their spirituality, education and skills. Clergy and lay team members on their part need to act with sensitivity and re-spect towards Readers as they adjust to new times. Above all the Church has no place for ministers who jealously guard a position of seniority for its own sake. Offering all due respect to those Readers who have kept abreast of the changes in the Church and with their own continuing training and personal development, it needs to be said for the health of the Church that all leadership is a supportive art to be learned throughout a lifetime and not to be confused with importance or a safe seat (see Walters 1992). Readers who are specialists in biblical studies are fully aware of how God is constantly calling them to discover newness in them-selves in the power of Jesus' Resurrection and as part of the process of being led into the fullness of the promises of the Kingdom (2 Cor. 5.17). In a trinitarian ecclesiology of difference in relationship there need be no concern about higher or lower status. A community of equals with different tasks can celebrate the value of Reader Ministry.

The Presiding Task: Mission and Eucharist

How is the parish priest to handle being both a member and being in charge, the captain of the team yet a playing member? There is so much to be learned about this difficult area. We can build up clues from many places. For example, in an aircraft it is the person actually at the controls who has final responsibility for that moment of the journey – *regardless of the presence of* more senior ranking officers. There are certainly parallels here in liturgical terms, in that whoever is leading a service is in charge for that occasion in the presence of others who may have more formal authority for parish life in general. How authority can be exercised in a dialogical way is the greatest issue to be faced about the future of collaborative ministry.

It may be argued that within the Trinity the Father does not seem to be truly equal with the Son and the Spirit because there is a sense in which he is alone the author of all things. However, it is essential to a social trinitarian understanding of God to realize that existence is by definition to be in relation. God's Fatherhood is impossible without the Son. There are no fathers without sons and no sons without fathers. The understanding of God as a communion of personal relations in which none is ever in a permanently dominating or dominated role, offers a vision for priesthood that manages to be 'in charge' without ever being merely separate or superior. But the frequent painful, practical experiences of this going wrong show how much more we still have to explore.

It can be considered perhaps as an unwritten mandate between priest and people. The priest is saying that the people must not forget that he or she is essentially one of the *laos*, a Christian like themselves, by baptism. Thankfully the people respond that they are glad this is his or her primary self-understanding but in fact they are asking the priest for the time being (in harmony with God and the bishop) to be the one who persuasively draws together and holds the values of their community. One metaphor for exploring the roles and qualities of priesthood required in one who presides is to consider the processes of discernment, blessing and witnessing. I shall move on now to expand on how I see these terms as a framework for describing the role of the parish priest for a new way of being Church.

Discernment

The local church has a basic need of wisdom or right judgement which is not a guaranteed condition for any human community. For the priest to be more than a guardian of traditional norms he or she will need to be committed to ways of growing in maturity as well as stimulating this in others. In the past we have tended to look to the clergy as the fount of all wisdom and as somehow closer to God than the rest of the Church – even though reality never really bore this out. Now the 'say one for me, vicar' mentality will have to go. The new approaches to initial and continuing training in which clergy, readers and laity – not to mention Local Ministry Teams – frequently train together, will produce a different church culture from the days of semi-monastic theological colleges as the place of formation for 'the' ministry. I am not introducing a polarization here between past and present. There were immensely valuable fruits in the previous patterns of training for priesthood but they cannot serve us now just as they used to. The context has moved on, human beings recognize different expectations in themselves, the Church has other agendas now. In short, because some parts of the picture have changed, everything has to be worked out afresh. This process will not take place by chance and not with everyone's approval. In practice there are now quite young ordinands whose own clerical role models – which triggered their sense of vocation – are looking to fulfil traditional expectations of self-sacrificial solo ministry. Transitions take many decades and other priorities will come well before one transition is complete. However the present need is to move from a ministry shaped by a high Christology to one that is eschatological-trinitarian, and the transition will require dioceses to make deliberate and tough choices about vision and policies.

WHAT KIND OF A PLACE IS THIS?
A church committed to being a sign and foretaste of God's passionate desire for creation will need to have its eyes and ears open to discern the nature of the place in which it is set. Although there are churches that by design or accident live in isolation from their locality – on grounds of purity of doctrine or lack of resources – it is one of the most frequently expressed ideas in discussions about mission today that there has to be listening attentiveness before any community or person may presume to formulate plans for the Kingdom in any given area.

The parish must ensure that somehow or other steps are taken so that the church knows what is going on in the wider neighbourhood and is recognized as sharing the concerns of local people. This attitude of companionship may be fostered through those members of the church who have time, energy, and the ability to know where to ask appropriate questions. Statistics about levels of deprivation are available through local authorities and some kind of basic population information is a necessary tool for any church with a share in mission for human wholeness.

The presiding minister also needs the courage to recognize and confront tendencies in the local church towards aspirations that are probably *not* Spirit-led. Sometimes the priest (with others) will be led to say 'Wait, let's examine whether this really is the way forward.' One priest joining a confident parish church with many active laity was under no doubt that the church was going somewhere and going fast – like a 125 intercity train. The question for his discerning ministry was 'To which destination is this train travelling?' It took a while for him to move up through the coaches to the front and have an input into deciding the route. It is the priest's responsibility to ensure that the church examines the effects of its policies and strategies and responds to its findings. A severe test of the priest-presiding gift comes when he or she is required to enable the church to wrestle with conflict and make a decision which will inevitably leave some members feeling angry or powerless. A maturing church will be struggling to share responsibility, including both the pain and the pleasure, for the overseeing of the missionary task and of the internal relatedness of the local church.

WHAT DOES GOD REQUIRE OF US?

Clergy now need the skills of adult educators and to themselves regularly engage in disciplined study. One major company recently suspected that its employees were not fully engaged with the enterprise – so much of their energy was going into hobbies, neighbourhood concerns and DIY. The management hit on the slogan 'Get your brains to work', implying that they wanted employees to be excited about the vision and practicalities of what they were supposed to be doing all day, rather than bored and clock-watching. To promote this they even provided everyone with a sum of money to pursue some course of study – anything, so long as it got their brains stimulated. Not all clergy need do Bible study, or read high powered academic theology –

though many more should than probably do. But there is theology everywhere and in everything – in the study of music, poetry, drama, history, politics, psychology, science and mathematics. The presiding priest needs to make time for study – along with time for family, for friends, for self – in short, for being human. If God is allowed constantly to reframe the Church's ministers in knowing who they are before him *as a person*, the rest will fall into place.

The local church must ensure that it finds the intellectual and emotional resources to keep up its energy flow in policy-making, planning liturgy, preaching, teaching, caring for the needy and evangelism. The priest, as the link with the catholic Church worldwide, must ensure that there are open channels to keep the local church in partnership with the movement of the Spirit. The reflective practitioner in ministry will enable the whole community to relate their daily responsibilities and hopes to the Word of God, the Eucharist and to communion with God in many kinds of prayer and concern for social action. The often inarticulate but bedrock theology of the laity needs to be brought out into the open and put to use as a vital resource.

The perennial question of how far the parish priest should expect to promote his or her own ideas and how far to listen to other viewpoints in matters of strategy is strongly related to the priest's own developing spiritual and intellectual quest. The corporate decisions and holistic agenda of a eucharistic community should be made out of the reflection and prayer of a local church that is prepared to give sufficient time to arriving at a consensus so that neither the priest nor some anarchic lobby within the church seeks to introduce a dominating authority by which to impose their views.

PRAYER AND WORSHIP THAT ENGAGES EVERYONE
It is in the eucharistic celebration – in word, preaching, intercession, reconciliation, peace, taking, offering, breaking and sharing bread and wine, reflecting and being sent out that the local church especially learns to be its true self. The ways in which the Eucharist is celebrated – the space, the furnishings, the human postures, the relationships, the voices, the vesture, the hopes and failings articulated – tell us about that local church's mission.

Every new celebration of the Eucharist is a fresh outpouring of God's blessing. Imaginative improvisations of poetry, drama, music, and colour can make real the Spirit's activity in different contexts, giving the Eucharist a 'superabundance of meaning' (Ford 1995). If we accept the Eucharist as the sacrament intended to help human beings grow up into the maturity of Christ, to be already growing in communion with God's life, then we should either recognize echoes of the trinitarian way of being or else make the necessary adjustments. This is what Paul means by discerning the body. It is the way the church prays and lives together – characteristically but not exclusively in the Eucharist – that enables the church to know, reveal and act out that peace which is God's final choice for the cosmos.

Clergy increasingly will be helping other members of the church to plan for and execute liturgies that will draw people into the mystery of God's life and will give them a place to ponder together the complex and often broken relatedness of human existence in the light of God's saving love (Ford 1995). Not denying the importance of good management in the Church, I am also reminded by R. S. Thomas of the utter mystery of the sacramental life of the Christian which it is particularly the priest's task to foster and open up. Thomas, in his poem *Hill Christmas*, speaks of the people staring

> into the dark chalice
> where the wine shone, felt it sharp
> on their tongue, shivered as at a sin
> remembered, and heard love cry
> momentarily in their heart's manger.

An important contribution by the parish priest will be honesty about his or her own partly redeemed and partly unrealized communication with God. Rather than being just a professional minister towards the rest of the church, the priest must be recognized as struggling with his or her own salvation and to be learning how simultaneously to be a member of the community as disciple, spouse, parent, and citizen. It is much harder now not to be able to hide anonymously behind the formalities of clerical role and instead to have to attempt an integration of person and role in a very public place. During this century gradually we are moving away from linking priestly ministry exclusively with a high Christology (Christ in glory) and a realized eschatology (the Church now is already God's Kingdom on earth). Above all we need clergy to be more self-aware so that they know as far as possible the effect they are having on people and situations – not patronizingly, assuming the right to talk while others listen, or to overrun the boundaries with no apology. There can be no collusion that either Church or ministry is already all that it should or could be. A growing-up church can acknowledge that and see its place in the world more sharply as a consequence.

In a church community focused on mission, the presiding minister will have a care for many issues great and small and must somehow have a feel for the entire enterprise – that is central to the priest's being there and is at the heart of the task. At the same time it involves everything both of the church's outreach and internal developing. There is a parallel with the trinitarian relatedness that is God. It is not in any one particular, but in the sum of them all in their mutual interrelatedness, that the heart of presiding rests. When the community gathers for the Eucharist, it is expressing its aspirations and receiving grace for its many-faceted share in God's mission.

The parish priest – and other priests in the ministry team – have the particular role of standing at the crossroads at the heart of the mission and Eucharist of the people of God. This is why they have been laid hands upon and set apart in a new relationship with God, the world, the Church and their friends. This is why it makes theological nonsense to suggest that the presidency at the eucharistic liturgy is merely one job among others which any member of the church may fulfil. It is not élitist or exclusivist to link priests alone with eucharistic presidency. This presidency cannot be separated from mission presidency. Anyone who holds together a local church in mission and ministry is a priest and the wider Church (with all the proper testing of vocation) should acknowledge this.

There is a practical aspect to this too. The priest with others needs to ensure that the Eucharist (and other worship) can speak truly to many differing occasions and groups of people. The possible improvizations are endless, but not boundariless. Part of the discerning ministry is to have a long-term and superb awareness of the Christian tradition of theology, spirituality, liturgy and practice. Only one who is utterly immersed in the tradition can keep it growing, imaginative, ever-fertile with new awakenings. Part of the ideal of former generations was to ensure stability through sameness. Every worship occasion employed the repetition of identical words, gestures and mood, with the priest deliberately effacing himself. The manuals and liturgical text books encouraged the repetition of the familiar.

It seems more appropriate in a postmodern era that worship should be the same and yet different every time. The metaphor of a jazz performance may be helpful. Every performance even of the same text will be new and different. To discern the limits of improvization requires intuitive experience and presiding at the Eucharist is not a matter for occasional duty. To deal with the heightening of emotion in worship requires all the maturity a priest can muster – and always in relation to other trusted church leaders to avoid self-delusion. Anyone who is in a position to preside regularly, through the standing which they hold in the local church, should be recognized as having a ministry within the wider catholic Church, should have this vocation tested by the Church, and be prayed over by a representative of that Church at a celebration of the Eucharist. The Church's name for this process and authorization is 'ordination'.

Blessing

The local church thrives through assurance of God's unlimited love. As Jesus gave a wedding feast absurd quantities of good wine, late in the proceedings, so we are to grow in the knowledge of God's overflowing blessing on creation. God continually acts creatively and redemptively inviting our response and sense of coresponsibility. The church is the place where we learn to cross a threshold of consciousness or make a leap to a new state of being. In the Eucharist, the heart of the church's life, we enjoy God's hospitality. God's people are gifted because of his nurturing and reconciling presence as Father, Son, and Spirit. In the Eucharist they learn how to live in and also live out God's life. African Christians in particular show how living in God's blessing is both a match for every act of violence against humanity but also the most authentic witness to the world.

When thousands have died of disease, when the rains have not come or when faced with genocide, their subversive acts of joyful celebration point others to their eschatological vision of a God who is present, acts and will act so that one day all will find their peace in him. The worship of the people of God is practising even now the joy and laughter of heaven for all creation.

None of this is dependent on the priest in the capacity of intermediary. Rather just as the whole baptized church is concerned to know and be a blessing in the context of God's desire for creation, the parish priest will seek to be a sign of God's blessing running through every aspect of the church's life. The Eucharist transforms the baptized community, through word, sacrament and relationships of loving intention into its truest self by fulfilling what God promises by inviting disciples to be 'in Christ'. The parish priest has a particular role in enabling the liturgical performance of sacramental acts that are blessings. Through the Spirit, and within the body of the church, they make real what they intend: baptism, Eucharist or reconciliation. In the eucharistic assembly and in worship, preaching, prayer and study, the triune God is blessed. There are also para-sacramental blessings, such as might be given to children by their parents, and by children to their parents or mutually between friends, spouses, or partners; there are many healings and intercession ministries; and there are pastoral, evangelical and serving ministries which for the eucharistic community are known as blessings from God. Mutual blessings come between God and his people when there is work undertaken for wholeness in the created order. All blessings now are a promise of that final state of blessedness when all things come together in Christ to be given, through the Spirit, into the hands of the Father.

Blessing is mutual affirmation possible through the communion we have with the life of the Trinity. In a frightening and scarred world it is one of the most significant gifts the Church can offer. To reassure people of their goodness and potential begins the process of creating the reality of their maturity – it is to set their feet on the path of their eschatological destiny. A blessing touches the original goodness of which Genesis speaks and calls forth persons and communities to be true to their vocation. Once we know our blessedness, we can be free to reassure others of theirs.

The priest's ministry of blessing requires the recognition of his or her primary task, not as being personally on the front line of mission all the time, but more humbly assisting others to recognize their own ministries and potential for growth. In this context the priest will be a resource: both as challenge and support.

Witnessing

The presiding priest will be called on to witness in two ways. First, together with a few others to be a channel for communication between the local church and partner churches as well as the rest of the Anglican Communion. The priest will attend synods, chapters and conferences where there will be a two-way process of listening and speaking, a reciprocal communication. Second, the priest will be witnessing to the community beyond the church and those on its fringes, as one (probably paid) who will have time to reflect on God's presence and activity, on the great issues people face – of life and death, hope in the face of tragedy, undeserved suffering. There will be some clergy who by temperament or in given situations for whom the personal testimony of their lives and conversation will be a primary element in their vocation. The image of the priest who 'picks his way Through the parish. . . limping through life on his prayers' (R. S. Thomas) under the gaze of the contented world still has its place. The 'parson-shaped hole' in the parish will not go away. However, increasingly the priest's task will be to empower others to understand their vital role of witnessing to Christ in their own spheres of influence. Where the priest's own expertise may often need to come to bear is in giving theological witness to the local church, gently but firmly probing old assumptions by asking whether the theological witness of the rest of the world Church supports or challenges accepted positions.

The local church focuses in one place the Church's catholic and apostolic witness to the possibility of redeemed or true human society and a reconciled world. Sharing in God's mission, the Church's task is to offer a fragmentary and partial sign and foretaste of the final destiny of all created life. God invites his Church to participate in creating a redeemed world where difference is respected and individuality is complemented by relationship. The priest in his or her own person and network of relationships is called particularly to be an honest and reliable signpost of that call to mature humanity which, in the Spirit, the Father offers to all who look to his Son in faith and hope.

Conclusion

Presidency is not the ideal term for carrying the full weight of what is meant by being a parish priest today – its history and overtones may make it completely impossible for some. I offer it – together with the three interrelated concepts of discernment, blessing and witnessing – as part of the journey towards a new model of Church. Anglican ecclesiology thrives on the cut and thrust of dialogue. We shall need a whole cluster of metaphors to explore the rich diversity of collaborative ministry.

5 ❧ WHO HAS POWER IN THE CHURCH?

Not everyone welcomes the vision for Local Ministry. There is a cluster of concerns. Partly, opposition is due to a nostalgia for the way things were. There seems to be a security in the old ways that many wish could be rediscovered and a fleeting hope that, by some miracle, money and ordinands will come along to bolster up the old understanding of church. This is to overlook the insight from systemic thinking that when one part of a whole changes there must inevitably be adjustments all round, otherwise pain and possibly disintegration will follow. In society generally, people's expectations of the way human organizations function are undergoing radical change. The term 'postmodernism' has been used to make the point that there is no going back. As the twentieth century draws to a close, even the Church must learn that the past cannot be rediscovered.

Finding meaning in a time of change implies that not all the answers are to hand. Like so many biblical people who entered desert experiences trusting in God to see them through, we will find new fruits and flowers which at present cannot even be conceived. Staying with the not knowing – guarding the chaos – is part of Christian vocation (Ward and Wild 1995).

Many genuinely recognize they are in a muddle about what 'local ministry' could mean. Yes, they accept that all members of the church are to take an interest in and share responsibility for the church's work in the parish and beyond. Yes, they approve of the attempt to discover the gifts of the Spirit to all members and the need to develop them to the full – but surely the laity are mainly to be concerned with ministry outside the parish. This assumption needs checking against the theology of the whole Church as a sign and foretaste of the eschatological times or against the proportion of people who in reality do go out of the parish each day to work. There are congregations today in which not a single person has paid employment.

There can be debate about what is 'local' – diocese, deanery, parish or something else? There is often surprise that a diocese could have a policy other than preaching the gospel. Rightly, there can be fears about accrediting a few laity to the detriment of the rest.

Necessary Management

Perhaps the most urgent set of reasons which have prompted me to take time to write this book are to do with the potential for disaster contained in Local Ministry strategies. I say this without detracting from my unwavering conviction that this is the most appropriate way forward for the Church of England at this time. The potential hazards are enormous for a Church which has a *laissez-faire* culture. By this I mean that present-day experience in dioceses, linked with loose authority structures, emphasizes that bishops and diocesan policies agreed at synods have only a minimal chance of influencing the development of the life of the parishes. Present discussions of the working conditions of Church of England clergy have highlighted the independence and freedom of clergy (and parishioners), except in the case of fla-grantly scandalous or wicked behaviour which prevents them from fulfilling their function in the local church. Whereas in the Roman Catholic Church since Vatican II there have been passion-ate pleas for more autonomy for the local church (usually mean-ing the diocese), in the Anglican Church the situation is almost the reverse. Diocesan Synods make resolutions and bishops make clarion calls with the sanguine knowledge that if fifty per cent of the parishes respond positively that is a good result.

Further, the expression 'management' is not often well re-ceived in the Church. Admittedly there is a debate as to whether 'management' refers to control and the steadying of dubious new enterprises or whether it means empowering and nerving new vision and opportunity. It seems to be a fair diagnosis that 'personal holiness' and 'spirituality' are generally preferred in church leaders as sounder than 'mere management', but in real-ity such a polarization can become a thinly disguised excuse for the perpetuation of a complacent and tranquillized ecclesial life-style. 'Holy management' is about promoting godly and mature Christian fruits in ways that make for healthy relationships and safe communities, assuming that conscientious overseeing both protects the vulnerable and develops the progress of the strong. It is an essential ingredient of Local Ministry, that every necessary step is taken to protect people from damage, whether participants in teams, congregations or the wider public.

Although the Church today is often isolated and ridiculed by practitioners of the human sciences, it has a long history of diligent pastoral care and an instinct for community work. However, modern standards in human caring properly highlight a lack of professionalism in churches regarding boundaries, supervision, confrontation and a sense of responsibility for the actions of accredited representatives. Observation suggests that the track record of churches when it comes to the early management of difficult relationships and inadequate standards of caring gives cause for deep and pervasive concern. Experience shows how trust is exploited and situations allowed to fester until a situation erupts into the realm of the unmanageable and dysfunctional, so that long-term, perhaps irreparable damage is done to many parties. The Anglican tradition of tolerance of inefficiency and lack of self-awareness, is incarnated in diocesan systems that 'permit' only a handful of overstretched bishops and archdeacons to 'manage' personnel or grapple with local church issues. Their lack of time and energy, because of so many disparate and questionable commitments, leads to many situations being left as long-burning fuses, either petering out in resentment and brokenness or erupting eventually in full-scale disaster.

Although many church leaders normally resist theology in favour of pragmatism, it will be a recurrent theme of this interpretation of the present situation that the absence of a Christian understanding of authority, power sharing, and order is precisely what disables the practice of ministry at many points.

All this, while sounding very negative, is intended to sound the alarm before it is too late regarding the new phenomenon of Local Ministry. At a time of financial stringency and when clergy numbers are in sharp decline, it is tempting for dioceses to reduce the size of their educational and management groups, to suppress archdeaconries and suffragan bishoprics and to cut or combine specialist or sector ministries with other work. I am making the strongest plea to ensure the recognition that new developments in collaborative ministry require powerful and genuine originality of thought and *more* rather than *less* educational and management support. In the light of the development of Areas of Collaborative Ministry – 'local churches' – there will be a vital new role for senior clergy in charge of a whole range of new ministries.

The self-identification of the Church of England as part of the One, Holy, Catholic, and Apostolic Church should never be left to chance. There is always an operational theology implied. Every decision taken or strategy adopted makes its claim for the character of the Church and the role it plays in society. What kind of Church God requires in any particular time and place is beyond partisan wranglings and the archaeological researching and rehearsing of old shibboleths, catholic, evangelical or liberal. If Local Ministry really is a *key* element in church policy for the next quarter of a century it needs maximum appraisal, review, and support. If this fails, what other strategy does anyone have to take its place?

A vital purpose of this book is to move significantly beyond the alternatives outlined above, in search of strategies of Local Ministry consistent with a God who is in essence relational and who cares for each person and who invites each local church to be a vehicle for God's own passionate agenda for the fulfilment and consummation of all creation.

Facing Some Anxieties about Local Ministry

Three issues frequently surface:

1. One of the chief difficulties which some people raise regarding the development of Local Ministry is to assume it is about the creation of a second-class order of local non-stipendiary clergy. Without hearing the whole argument, commonly people oppose such a vision. Such opposition would be entirely justified if that really was all that Local Ministry is about. In fact the House of Bishops' regulations rightly insist on an unbreakable relationship between such local ordained ministry and groups of laity. Parishes may enter by one of two doors. Either they may perceive a need for more priests – in which case they must be told to establish a lay ministerial team first. Or else, they may

want to set up a local team of laity and only possibly at a later date consider whether more ordained persons are required. In the context of a trinitarian understanding of church, talk of first and second class disappears – difference in relation leads to a radical reappraisal of all our inherited views of hierarchy.

2. Another objection to Local Ministry is that precisely at the time when laity in general are being encouraged to recognize their gifts and responsibility for ministry, there is being introduced a superior breed of laity who will absorb the ministry of others. This could not be further from the truth. All ministry today must be understood as belonging to the Church. No one possesses a ministry in isolation, or over against others, or even superior to others. Some will have more responsibility for focusing, leading, co-ordinating, encouraging, and empowering their brothers and sisters – because the community calls them for the time being for this purpose. But the John the Baptist principle applies to all ministry, 'He must grow greater, I must become less' (John 3:30). No one is called to work so hard as to take the place of another. No one is dispensable. The Local Ministry Team, acting as an expanded or exploded version of the inherited model of the priest alone, is not there to replace the ministry of others. Rather it is there to ensure that the community has all the ministry it needs to ensure the effective mission which is the responsibility of the entire Christian community.

3. Again, there are justified fears that the role of the Parochial Church Council might be undermined by Local Ministry Teams. Recognizing this potential hazard, those who make arrangement for establishing teams must, at every stage, teach and demonstrate that the relationship will be one of a creative partnership. In all probability membership will overlap and at regular intervals there will be a need for the relationship between the two bodies to be appraised and adjusted. This will be one of the important functions of diocesan Local Ministry Officers, who can take an objective view. Even with the most careful

educational, spiritual, and jurisdictional support and challenge, there are many areas where a Local Ministry Scheme could result in conflict and pain for the local church and individual members, not to mention members of the public. But in themselves these are not objections to careful experiment and reflective practice, but a challenge to founding such new developments on adequate theology and with sufficient confidence and consideration to take care for all concerned.

What is the solution? As I have already suggested several times, a new model of shared decision-taking is required. The difficulties only just begin to arise when a priest and local congregation make the decision to commit themselves to collaborative ministry. 'We're all for change, so long as it makes no difference.' How in reality do professional itinerant clergy begin to share responsibility and decision-taking with non-stipendiary clergy, Readers and laity? How do volunteers and paid staff collaborate? If in the new dispensation the vicar genuinely wants to sit down with others and reach a decision that all can own, what does he or she do with inherited anxieties such as 'What will the bishop make of this?' 'What happens if the people want something I can't go along with, or which reflects a theology I find unacceptable?'

A good example to make the point would be baptism policy. This has a long-running success rate in raising the temperature of any Church of England gathering. Supposing that a new priest has just arrived in a parish and rapidly develops an uneasiness about the inherited baptism policy or lack of one. From that critical point of realization onwards there is a whole cluster of possibilities. What will happen next? I have used this example as a test case in workshops on new styles of ministry, where the issues for discussion include the following:

Clergy Appointments

In the first place the situation, common enough, begs questions about the appointment of parish clergy. The present process is more complex than when the bishop alone took responsibility for moving clergy from A to B. Now there is a delicate dance of authority in which at least five people or groups have a right to participate: the specially appointed parish representatives, the archdeacon, the patron, the candidate and increasingly his or her complex family networks. Once in the early days of Local Ministry a senior and outspoken incumbent threatened at a synod that if ever he came into a parish with such a scheme he would dismantle it within a fortnight. Fifteen years ago he received humorous assent for his remark. Today more of his hearers would be asking why he had gone to a parish where he did not respect what the local people had been working for in the previous few years. Yes, of course, any new priest will want to challenge and work for adjustments, but it no longer seems appropriate to begin on day one as though his arrival signals the opening of an entirely new chapter in that parish's life. The inherited terminology 'vacancy' and 'interregnum' to describe the period after the retirement or move of one until the arrival of the next parish priest is in urgent need of replacement. Many parishes thrive during a vacancy only to sink back into dependency later. There may be a valuable degree of liminality – lack of clear identity, direction and order – between clergy appointments but never an absence of ministry or leadership. Learning to 'guard the choas' (Ward and Wild 1995) is pivotal to the maturing of Christian community life.

What Degree of Trust is Possible?

The vicar in the case study who disapproves of the baptism policy in his or her new situation could attempt to declare UDI and simply alter the practice, as though it were entirely a personal, professional matter. Or else the matter could be aired at the Parochial Church Council with a view to persuading others of the vicar's own view. If this failed, the vicar would have to decide what degree of compromise was possible. Another way forward, often observed, would be for the parish priest to take into his or her confidence an inner core who reach a compromise agreement, but whether by accident or design fail to communicate this clearly, leaving everyone else struggling to know what is really going on. Again, the vicar's views might meet with such warm recognition that a whole process of meetings and statements could be negotiated. A good end would be a PCC decision which was owned and celebrated as parish policy, rather than just what our present vicar wants. However, at the heart of the issue is the question of who decides what is essentially an ecclesiological matter? Is there a deanery ecumenical or diocesan policy – unlikely! What kind of a church admits children and adults into its membership in this or that way? What possible variations are there in preparation and liturgy? What understanding of God is at work?

The Painful Path to Handling Conflict

Most Anglicans today will give lip service to the theology and practice of shared ministry in the Church, but are at a loss when it comes to ways of thinking this through radically and carefully. This is not just a matter of theory. Far from it. How much emotional pain is caused to churches and damage to persons through a lack of clarity about the vital significance of working for a shared theology, and for knowing how to harness conflict and to understand power relations. In one parish where the vicar and a group of dedicated laity attempted a new style of collaboration enormous anger was eventually generated by the vacillation of the priest between being 'member of the team' and 'autocratic dictator'. As some of the laity agreed, they knew how to work with a clerical dictator – they had lots of experience of the priest assuming authority and taking responsibility for everything. The laity who choose to work with such a priest know when to nod assent. Those who want to argue or put another view eventually run out of steam or are marginalized by the rest for rocking the boat. Churches on the whole are not well equipped for handling controversy. Those who side with the vicar generally hold the trump card. It is vital for clergy and indeed any church leaders and members to offer new thinking and ideas. However, it is painful and confusing if new messages about collaboration are beamed from the vicarage but are not accompanied by consistent and patient negotiation and consultation leading to trust and acceptance. The researches of George Wilson, a Jesuit who does church consulting with Management Design Institute in Cincinnati, Ohio, suggest that leaders who take genuine pains to listen respectfully to the concerns of local people are rewarded with the permission to present new challenges for the future (Wilson 1993).

A Church that models its community life on the Trinity will be aiming for 'the asceticism of trust, mutuality and love' (Byrne 1993). This has implications for working for structures that allow for the costly conversion to a culture of mutual listening. Gillian Fraser SSC argues that an essential element in becoming community is the 'relaxed hard work' of mutual reconciliation, and encouragement in the journey of faith (Fraser 1993). This process takes time; it means getting less done; it is, however, of the essence of the task of a Church rooted in the Trinity. Its way of doing business and of dealing with relationships is a vital part of its proclamation of Jesus and his Kingdom.

An unpredictable mix of both a traditional and a new way of priest and people relating is common in my experience – inevitably in a time of transition – but still extremely disheartening for all concerned and in really bad cases a poor witness to the wider community.

A Workable Model of Shared Authority

So, what tools are available to learn the art of collaborative decision-taking? Colleagues in business, education, government and voluntary organizations are struggling with these issues and their published wisdom and conferences are a resource for the Church. A judicious blend of the disciplines of philosophy, systems-thinking, and theology can, I believe, offer helpful frameworks of reference for grappling with these vital but elusive questions of authority.

The Urgent Need for a Shared Ministry that Works

Many church members are bewildered, frustrated, not to say undernourished because of the situation in their church. Laity often complain that the clergy are not themselves concerned to develop strategies and do not 'allow' initiatives to be taken by others; nor will they 'permit' house groups, nor lay-led services; nor will they engage openly with the ideas of others, especially if they are likely to lead to conflict with their own particular brand of Christianity. All too often none of us has the humility to see how small is our own insight into God and therefore how much it needs to be placed side by side with those of many others. It is as though we went down on to a beach at midnight claiming to see the entire ocean, armed only with a torch. In fact our understanding of God, vital and deep as it may be, is only partial and is for mutual sharing with others.

Clergy often claim to be protective of older members of the congregation who like a rumbling volcano are said not to tolerate changes in music or the involvement of children. Such developments it is said will lead to them staying at home or more threateningly, ceasing to contribute to the income. Many clergy and Readers are suspicious of the developing power of the laity, believing, accurately as it happens, that this will mean the end of the Church as we know it. So, who has the power in the Church?

New Testament Resources

The first response might be that it is God who has power in the Church, but so often what is experienced is the apparent impotence and absence of God. What does society see of the God we claim to be in charge of the world and who puts everything in subjection to Christ? The New Testament admits that this power is not yet seen (Heb. 2:8) and that God's power appears strongest in weakness (2 Cor. 12.9). The paradoxical power of the cross is what properly belongs to every community of Jesus Christ and to every ministry and office. The Hymn to Christ in the Letter to the Philippians (Phil. 2.6–11) is appropriate material for meditation for any who would perform a task in the Church, that is, to share the work of him who has been given a name above every name – *Kyrios*, Lord – to the glory of God the Father. It is one of the earliest stated Christ beliefs that Jesus Christ is Lord (through the Holy Spirit) (1 Cor. 12.3). Paul states that this is what is specific to being a Christian community as opposed to any other mystery cult or religion. It is also the personal confession of each Christian.

All churches have the binding characteristic of placing themselves freely under the authority of Christ's ever-present resurrection power. The New Testament states repeatedly that Christ is present in the local church – to the close of the age (Matt. 28.20b). His active help, rather than static presence in ritual, is what offers to the church forgiveness, hope, and a sense of purpose. The gospels show that Jesus' teaching, healing, forgiveness and driving out of demons is as God's representative. Only God has such power – therefore each person is left to decide whether the ministry of Jesus to him or herself is from heaven or from man (Matt. 11.2–6; Luke 7.18–23).

Fundamentally in the New Testament, power in Christ's church is understood as *diakonia*, not *arché*. There is no discussion of 'hierarchy'. Paul describes himself as 'servant / minister of Jesus Christ, called to be an apostle' (Rom. 1.1). The apostle stands chiefly in a relationship of ministering, as a servant towards his master. Instead of a relationship of superiority or inferiority the Church has a different model. It is that of a willingness to minister out of deference to one's brothers and sisters, quite freely and without ambition or claim to status.

The type of this service is the human ministry of Jesus grounded in *diakonia* (Mark 10.42–45; Matt. 20.28; see also Luke 22.25–27; John 13.1–17). It is the whole work of Christ, centred on the cross, that informs the conduct of the local church about selection for and exercising 'ministry'. Paul points this out to the church at Corinth (1 Cor. 3.5) and shows how it is intended as the means of reconciliation not merely for the Church but for the entire world (2 Cor. 5.18–19). Paul also insists that the local church must not become dependent on their leaders in ministry, but become responsible and accountable together (see 1 Cor. 3.1–4). Further, what is said of the body of Christ (1. Cor. 12.1–3, 4–11, 12–31; Rom. 12.4ff.) taken with what is said of spiritual gifts, is central to the ministry of responsibility, freedom and self-accountability of the Christian community. No member of the church may claim to be independent; none may be described as unnecessary. 'To each is given manifestation of the Spirit for the common good '(1 Cor. 12.7). Every Christian community member shares in the power of Christ equally but differently and without egotism and rivalry. This is why the more excellent way is that of love that is not sentimental but strong, exact, simple, practical and self-effacing (1 Cor. 13).

Dialogue with Theories of Power

Experience tells me that to belong to a church is to become involved in any number of power relations which can be very complex. Yet I constantly meet clergy and laity who are leaders in local churches who react violently to any suggestion that their work has anything to do with authority or power. A healthy sense of humility and their own unworthiness, together with the strictures of Jesus against lording it over people, rightly check church people from adopting undue force. What can be more problematic, however, is the failure to recognize that if the exercise of authority is not worked at at the conscious level, a vacuum will inevitably be filled somehow or other. Perhaps part of the difficulty is a failure both to distinguish between the terms 'authority' and 'power', and to maintain an outmoded understanding of the idea of 'power' itself.

If we take the latter first, it is a frequently expressed idea that 'power' is an abstract property which by fair or foul means a minority within a society have taken possession of, for the benefit or to the disadvantage of the remainder. So, for example, wealthy or land-owning minorities, or professional élites with access to knowledge, information, and communication systems are described as 'powerful' in contrast to the others, who on this analysis are robbed of power. There is no denying the feelings being articulated here – anger and resentment by a majority at the hold which the 'powerful' have over their lives. Quite definitely, many people act as though they were constrained by being the fixed or static subject to others who are the object, and vice-versa.

The time has come for the Church to break through to a new level of consciousness and a more Spirit-filled concept of power. Instead of thinking of power as based on inequality, suppose we took a view that is essentially relational. Our trinitarian basis for thinking about the nature of Church must imply that power and love must be closely kept together and that a fundamental aim of our faith is to build up the power of everyone in 'circles of influence, mutual healing, a process of interaction' (Donovan 1982).

It is helpful that Michel Foucault, the French philosopher, suggests we look in another place for a productive definition of power and in so doing offers a vital tool for recognizing the potential for all to take hold of the levers of power. His rather gruesome, detailed studies of the language and practice of education, public surveillance, treatment of delinquency, interrogation, imprisonment, reform, torture, and capital punishment (1977) offer a way of discourse concerning power that moves away from the commonly received notions. Instead of conceiving of power as some 'thing' possessed by one and therefore not by another, Foucault points to the constantly fluctuating networks of relationship and roles that exist to make organizations function. He argues that apart from all the contributions of individual experts, say to the work of a university, there has to be an overall 'idea' or unifying concept for the administrators, professors and students to work with or react against. It is not, however, the idea itself that governs whether or not the university functions satisfactorily, but the system of rules and organization that carry the values which determine what kind of university this will be at this particular time. Rules of discourse, as Foucault calls them, have a vital role in establishing a given system of relations. Talking about what kind of institution we are aiming to be, he claims, is both dependent on and yet feeds back and influences the everyday patterns of the organization.

The implications for a church are easy to see. An inherited view is that bishops and parish clergy and a few statesmanlike laity (men and women) have the entire system stitched up. Power in this view of things properly belongs to some and not to others. To enter into committed membership of such a church is to accept this nondiscursive practice as a given, even as having the authority of the New Testament and the witness of history. However, recent theological reflection on the nature of the Church invites a fresh examination of power and of authority – the permission to exercise power and the style with which to do so.

The present-day concept of baptism in international ecumenical discussion points to the whole Christian community having the right and responsibility to take hold of the networks and conversations by which church power becomes active and effective in mission and ministry. Where many are not at present feeling powerful, there is an urgent need to give them authority or permission to take up what is rightfully theirs. This is where Foucault's insights about institutions may be of value. If power be imagined as the space between people, the dynamic networks of communication, open to distortion, abuse and domination, or openness, honesty and collaboration, we could say that they are in a sense neutral until someone puts their mark upon them. However, in the case of an institution like the Church of England, centuries of expectation create both arrogant claims that the Church owes its shape to direct divine intervention and also the assumption that some are automatically to be in a position of subordination or of superordination. On the one hand there are the young, the elderly, those with a mental or physical handicap, those with poor educational attainment, women, and those who are known to have broken the core ethical norms. Though even as I look at this list, I recognize how complex expectations are in different places; also that precisely those who are apparently marginalized, in a voluntary organization have enormous power to manipulate the system and so, in the old understanding wield enormous power. On the other hand (and again this is more complex than it seems) bishops, archdeacons, clergy, wealthy laity, and senior figures in the institutions of education can be 'powerful' figures in the Church.

There is a strong move in today's Church towards empowering every church member to recognize and utilize their opportunity and gifts in the service of God's enterprise, the fulfilment of the entire creation, within which the Church has a place of particular discernment and responsibility. However, progress towards this end is held back by senior figures who do not subscribe to the current theological drive or whose personality will not easily permit them to face the consequences in practical terms. Also the fact that people rarely join a religious institution in order to change it, but prefer the *status quo,* means that immature dependency on the part of laity remains a strong characteristic of the Church of England. However, within the present-day account of the Church's dynamic rooted in *communion* there is an urgent need to recognize the limits and the potential of the responsibility of all concerned to make effective the field of relationality which is the Church.

Part of this must be the recognition that certain people are called upon to have a more prominent role because of their competence, knowledge and terms of appointment. Further, particular individuals will have varying, twinned, and overlapping roles and any serious analysis of the deployment of power networks will be naive not to take note of this given and fluctuating complexity. We are talking truly here of how to handle and make decisions, in conditions of relation among difference and where all have permission to contribute and to either promote or exclude causes of action in the life of the Church.

This is not the place to develop scholarly debate on the success or failure of Foucault's complex analyses. What may perhaps be usefully drawn from his work on the economy of power relations are his insights about antagonisms:

- He suggests that observation of anti-authority struggles (regarding, for example, opposition to the power of men over women, of parents over children or of bureaucracy over how people live) centre on the status of the individual. There is conflict between the right of individuals properly to claim the right to be truly and independently themselves, and any stance that seems to split up community life or sever bonds with others. How to be different and yet together is the fundamental issue.
- Second, many contemporary issues about authority focus on the abuse of privilege which comes with élitist knowledge, competence, or qualification. Here there is suspicion of secrecy or the potential for mystifying situations to the detriment of others. The close connection between knowledge and power is under the spotlight.
- Third, modern anti-authoritarian questions want to check out the relationship between my right to be me over against the determinism of violent statements about me made on grounds of economy and ideology.
- In summary, Foucault concludes, 'the main objectives of these struggles is to attack not so much "such or such" an institution of power, or group or élite, or class, but rather a technique, a form of power.'

Where it seems there may be clues for working on the local church's use and abuse of power networks is in recognizing with Foucault how power exists within the detailed arrangements of a complex institution. So in a church the exercise of power is to be read off, for example, in the way space is used – liturgically for clergy and laity, or in seating patterns at church meetings. Power is to be observed in the meticulous arrangements (both conscious and unconscious) for communicating between groups and organizing events, and in the articulated or unspoken regulations that govern its internal life. Divide and rule is fit and well in the Church as an unspoken principle behind unnecessary secrecy or just poor lines of communication. Also to be taken into account are the range of events which are 'allowed' by 'the management' to be part of that particular church's activity.

What I take from Foucault is that power does not exist as an *entity*, but only when it is put into action. In terms of church organization, the dynamics of power are always a demonstration of the agreement, explicit or tacit, about relationships between all concerned. The opposite of power in action is not the response of someone acted upon, but passivity, the failure to activate power. Power is in this analysis the entire field of activity and relationships that make the Church. So the activation of power is not to be feared or rejected, rather the opposite. Assertiveness and energetic disagreement are part of love and life. What is in question is the permission to make power work, the authority of everyone to take part and the quality of that involvement. Where the exercise of power is distorted we see the misuse of authority to rob others of their freedom, dignity, expectation of being treated with courtesy, or to paralyse the proper reciprocity of interrelationship. The Church must attend, therefore, to all styles of exercising power which are motivated by fear, domination, servitude, violence, adversarial competition, a static and mechanistic view of relations, or the destruction of individual characteristics. We need leaders – clerical and lay – who have no need to be protected from bold but courteous controversy.

Dialogue with Systems Thinking

In the mainstream churches there are erratic signals about the importance of engaging with burgeoning theories about the practice of management. I share the view that it would be possible for the Church of England to take on board a vast amount of insight from these areas – flexibly, intelligently and without losing touch with theological and spiritual rigour. There is only space here to trace the outlines of some of the thinking in secular disciplines with which church managers should be in touch.

In December 1993 and February 1994 I took part in a work-centred consultation organized by Avec, at that time a service agency for church and community work based in London. The resources of Avec, its books and occasional papers relating the churches and community development, have now been transferred to the Wesley and Methodist Studies Centre, Westminster College, Oxford. Two staff members and five professional church managers worked together in two five-day sessions with a three-month interval between. We recognized at the outset that our work ministries were all different, but that we could help each other and learn from each other if we gave ourselves whole-heartedly to the process. Essential ingredients were a willingness to enter into the situations of each other person in the context of a temporary Christian base in which we shared principles and inspiration.

In the first part of the consultation we described our work experience in written papers so that each could see the situations of the others. We worked to establish a creative tension between our past stories and traditions, present needs and opportunities and possibilities of the future. In the three months between the two parts of the consultation we had time for sharing the process with our colleagues back at work as well as to test out for ourselves the reality of some of the early discussion. During week two we designed solution strategies and set criteria for success. This was followed by planning in more detail and considering what materials and support from other people we would need as we implemented and adjusted our solutions effectively.

During the consultation we pondered on the value for ourselves and the whole Church of systems thinking, recognizing social processes, learning good habits of leadership, the quality of interaction and performance when people work together in synergy, assertiveness, creative management of the self, models of problem-solving, confrontation skills, the need for generative learning, the integration of feelings with ideas, or bringing about a closure on discussion.

I found the group process was encouraging. Working together helped participants to see what was really going on in some difficult parts of the work as well as in providing tools to work with in new situations in the future. It was particularly important that the staff members modelled the integration of holiness and management – conversation flowed easily between the disciplines, not least biblical study and theology. Further there was no sense of lifting theories from another world – that say of managing multinational corporations and 'applying' them to the local church. Rather, as a context or set of problems emerged in group discussion, the idea would be gently floated that such and such a writer or theory could usefully be drawn into the conversation at this point. This called for consultants who could listen and who knew the writings of several disciplines well enough to bring them out or keep silent as appropriate. The use of diagrams to represent communally what was being said proved irritating and distracting to some of us. Personally, most of the time, I found they allowed everyone to own the way the discussion was travelling and to be able, visually, to see how it had emerged and developed. Clearly a great deal would depend on the skill and integrity of the person charged with charting the group conversation.

For those who wish to follow up this approach to management in the Church, a valuable introduction is provided in George Lovell's *Analysis and Design* (1995). He encourages all church leaders and communities to think practically, theoretically and theologically about the complex human processes in which we take part daily. The experiences of individuals and groups working for the Kingdom of God in mission and ministry can be enlightened and enhanced by dialogue with the behavioural sciences and principles of adult education.

One of the particular benefits for me was to explore the theories of Peter M. Senge (1993). I discovered how all churches could see themselves as learning organizations. Taking this approach would lead to the exploration of the following five key ideas which should be much further developed for the clarity and health of the life of the churches:

- A Growing Concern for Discipleship
  Increasingly laity want the Church to recognize the importance of a developing spiritual journey possible for everyone, whatever their gifts, and which takes seriously their individual uniqueness. Further they want a church practice that wel-

comes all ages and rejoices to integrate their differing contributions. All appointments to leadership in the churches should spring from a clear discernment of a commitment to discipleship.

- A Holistic Rationality

  Taking into account feelings and particular contexts, as well as the intellect, there is a move among laity to want to understand the faith and to make connections with their occupation and the way society is ordered.

- A Shared Vision

  In all the organizational networks of the churches there is movement towards a shared mission statement and aims and objectives to make this effective. This is related to the passionate concern of God for the wholeness of creation and is resourced not only from the past (the Scriptures, tradition, history and so forth) but also by a knowledge of the trinitarian God's final intentions for the kaleidoscopic wholeness of all things.

- Team Learning

  Instead of individuals in ministry, there is a profound move towards teams of all kinds of ministers, learning, worshipping and working in mutual strength and vulnerability. This is moving towards a Church *of* rather than *for* people.

- Seeing the Whole

  Churches are moving towards seeing themselves as complex and open systems, engaging with the triune God and the entire world. It is no longer regarded as appropriate either to remain separate from other parts of the local and world Church or to blame others when things do not work out.

Conclusion

At a time when the Church's influence in society is probably waning in most situations, it is appropriate that Christians should be asking questions about the honest facing of power issues. How do structures work to the advantage of all? Do we want to be led by senior clergy with over-full diaries and lives dominated by an impossible workload? The prospect of a never-ending increase of compulsive one-way management is appalling. It does not work; it leads to barely concealed anger on all sides. Where is the trinitarian God in all this? We need structures for the future which will speak to church members and society of a gospel of self-worth, mutual trust, tenderness, openness, and a holistic balance between achieving and letting be – the integration of gentleness and strength. In some ways secular insights about this exercise of organizational and personal power relations are leaving the Church behind. It is dishonest and manipulative to suggest that leaders do not sometimes have to be directive. We need vision and new ideas as well as collaborative decision-making and action. An urgent agenda for all churches today, therefore, must be to pursue questions about planning, objectives, evaluation, control, motivation, supervision, leadership and power, policy-making, boundaries, change, conflict, roles, stress (systemic and personal) and communication.

If we are serious about moving towards a new model of Church – without necessarily knowing *how* to get there – we could ponder Schillebeeckx' suggestion of the paradigm of humanity (Church with a human face). He observes, 'A religion which in fact has a dehumanizing effect, in whatever way, is either a false religion or a religion which understands itself wrongly' (Schillebeeckx in King 1995). It is time for Christians to look again at their 2,000 years of resources for a new vision of church authority that gives freedom, dignity and value to every person.

6 & KEYS TO GOOD PRACTICE IN LOCAL MINISTRY

Identifying 'Local Ministry'

At the 1994 Edward King Institute for Ministry Development Consultation good practice in Local Ministry was identified in the following terms:

  (i) Each member of the local church is aware of their true worth.

 (ii) There is a common sense of calling to share in the ministry of the local church.

(iii) There is a continuing process of discernment of people's gifts, and of the opportunities to exercise them, both in the church and in the local community.

(iv) The local context and culture is taken seriously as a place where people are loved by God, and Local Ministry sets out to meet the needs of the local community.

 (v) A common vision is worked out, and there is clarity about expectations, developing roles and commitments.

(vi) There is regular planning, prayer, reflection and review, and an openness with one another that involves enjoyment and risk.

(vii) The local church leaders are responsible for ensuring that gifts are exercised in such a way as to encourage others in developing their ministry, and not 'de-skill' them.

(viii) The developing patterns of ministry are 'owned' by the whole congregation and rooted in prayer and fellowship.

(ix) Adequate oversight and appraisal is provided both from within and beyond the local church.

 (x) The diocese is involved in affirming, training and monitoring Local Ministry.

Making Local Ministry Work –
and Keeping it Working

The wisdom of the Edward King Institute 1994 Consultation was that:

(i) The selection of Local Ministry Teams is a joint process involving the active participation of both the local church and the diocese. One group spoke of a 'team chosen, owned and understood by the local church and recognized and accredited by the diocese'. 'The process of selection needs to be owned by both the local church and the wider Church.' The role of the local church in calling people out needs to be emphasized as an aspect of vocation that has been forgotten compared with the expectation of an individual offering himself or herself.

(ii) Central to the planning of training is that 'the team (lay and clergy) undergo formation and training together'. Training needs to be 'effective in integrating laity and clergy'.

(iii) The diocese has a vital role in the planning and provision of training. How this is designed and delivered is discussed in the next section, but groups pointed out that it is essential that training takes account of each local context.

(iv) With regard to licensing, there was general support for the idea that this should be for a fixed term, although one group suggested there was a need for research to find out what would be lost by this. The process of licensing needs to make clear the expectations about the role and commitment of those being licensed.

(v) Continuing training of the whole team together, lay and clergy, and regular review with people from outside the team participating were seen as important in maintaining the health of the Local Ministry Team.

(vi) One issue that emerged as particularly important was the induction of new clergy, particularly incumbents, into existing teams. A number of 'horror stories' of the damaging consequences of the arrival of a new incumbent were told.

It was clear from these that some clergy find it difficult to appreciate the distinctive nature of Local Ministry Teams and the changes they themselves need to make in their attitudes and practice if they are to be able to work with such teams. Those appointing them would seem to have found it difficult to assess their capacity to change and to convey the distinctiveness of the situation into which they were going.

(vii) The appointment, training and induction of clergy into existing teams clearly needs to be a carefully managed process. The use of an external consultant to work with them and their teams during the early months after their arrival was recommended.

Developing Constructive Relationships between the Local Church and the Diocese

The relationship between the local church (area of collaborative ministry), the parish or the benefice, and the diocese and national bodies emerged as an important issue at an early stage in the 1994 Consultation. Groups were talking about 'the local and the catholic' and 'bottom–up and top–down' and 'local initiative and diocesan support'. A constructive working relationship between these two is a major factor in the healthy development of local ministry. Members of the Consultation saw the diocese as having a key role in stimulating and encouraging Local Ministry, but wished to preserve an emphasis on local initiative.

In one diocese it was reported that a working party on Local Ministry had visited a number of different areas with Local Ministry Teams and listened to their experience. In this process it had gained confidence and learned to investigate and ask more searching questions of these teams. From this experience it had become able to visit other places with a knowledge of the issues that need to be raised and worked through.

One suggested model takes this shape:

- Parishes offer their projected scheme.
- The diocese recognizes this and appoints a consultant for each parish.

- The consultants work with the parish in developing their scheme.
- The diocese is able to monitor these developments through the consultants.
- Over a period of time it is possible to identify a 'core curriculum' for the training of Local Ministry Teams.
- Parishes are able to select modules of training to suit their own needs.
- Training on working together as a team or group is essential for all.

Key elements in the role of the diocese include:

(i) Promoting the idea of Local Ministry Teams and stimulating parishes to think about their own ministry.

(ii) Providing resources, including training, people with expertise to work with emerging Local Ministry Teams, and finance for deprived areas, e.g. Urban Priority Areas.

(iii) Sharing in the process of selecting people for Local Ministry Teams.

(iv) Moderating their training and development.

(v) Authorizing and licensing them.

Good practice in Local Ministry Teams involves them in 'contributing to and receiving from the wider Church' and 'drawing on the resources, strength and wisdom of the diocese' (Edward King Institute 1994).

Enabling the Church to Change

The Edward King Institute 1994 Consultation examined the issues raised by the culture of the Church and its resistance to change. From their experience of introducing local ministry, delegates drew up a series of guidelines for introducing change:

(i) The first is to value and affirm what already exists in the congregation and the community, to appreciate their history and the factors that have made them what they are.

(ii) Consultation at an early stage of those who may be affected is essential. This needs to be done long before there are any plans or proposals. This process needs to give people opportunities to express their feelings. Genuine consultations may have the result that people express suspicion, hostility or anger. It is important that if the idea of change arouses these feelings, they are expressed and faced, and not avoided. If the truth of people's feelings is not recognized it may lead to an unhealthy resentment which undermines the development of Local Ministry. If there should be a great deal of anger at this stage, a 'cooling-off time' may be needed.

(iii) The best approach to adopt is to invite those who are involved to develop their own proposals and to help them to work them out. Alternative ways forward should be invited. Throughout the process, wherever the suggestions and proposals come from, it is important to work at enabling the people involved to *own* the ideas that are being developed.

(iv) It is often a positive way forward to arrange for congregations to be addressed by people from other places who have found Local Ministry helpful in their own situation.

(v) Throughout this process personal contact is important. Spending time with individuals, offering support to those who are threatened by the changes that are being proposed, and encouragement to those who can see their value but are hesitant to commit themselves, has a major influence on the readiness of congregations to take the risk of embracing a new and unfamiliar pattern of church life.

(vi) An approach which works at gaining people's trust through the open sharing of information, efforts to help them grasp what is being suggested and a readiness to accept their hesitation, anxiety and pain, is far more likely to be effective in the long run.

(vii) Time is a crucial element. Proposals that are hurried through are likely to unravel later. The speed of change needs to be monitored.

(viii) The process of *decision making* needs to be as transparent as possible. People need to be clear where authority and responsibility for taking decisions lies. They need a grasp of the relationship between the local unit and the diocese.

(ix) Finally, the whole process needs to be rooted in *prayer*. Suggestions can be made to help people to pray, for example prayer leaflets. They need to be helped to pray for the whole life of the community not just for the church, so that an ethos that is appropriate to Local Ministry is developed. Prayer in the middle of meetings, not just at the beginning or the end, and special times of prayer are worth considering.

Lay Presidency at the Eucharist?

The debate about lay people having permission to preside at the Eucharist is related to Local Ministry and is gathering momentum especially among laity. Honest discussion, as free as possible from defensiveness and protection of clergy status, is vital.

Certainly one of the urgent issues the Church of England will face over the next generation or so is how to match the need for Sunday celebrations of Holy Communion with the ever-decreasing number of available clergy. At present there can be as many as half a dozen Eucharists taking place in a widespread rural benefice on a Sunday – not to mention the services of partner denominations in the same locality. In some places an alternative to expecting a solo priest to preside at them one after the other has been lay people licensed to administer from the reserved sacrament or a Reader leading the service of the Word until the priest's car speeds to the vestry door. Those who already administer the reserved sacrament at public worship do so with great care and are respected in this ministry. It becomes extremely important to them and seems to be an affirmation of the local for the congregation. It is striking what hurt is caused when such a policy is reversed by a bishop or new parish priest.

Talking with others in a number of dioceses I sense a strong dis-ease about these piecemeal arrangements. However, in a Church that wants to be open to the whole community there need to be a wide variety of praise, prayerful and teaching services, including the celebration of Holy Communion. Certainly in the Church of England during this century there has been a powerful move towards establishing the Eucharist as the main act of Sunday worship for committed Christians. These can be planned and led by a team of clergy, Readers and laity. There can be worship in every church (at the same time if required) leaving people locally free to choose things they will be part of.

The theological wisdom of the mainstream Christian tradition so far and of the present time is that presiding at the Eucharist is the work of the one who is recognized locally as the ordinary focus of leadership in mission and ministry. This could be the stipendiary priest for the group of parishes in which any particular eucharistic gathering is taking place, one of the other priests who regularly is involved in that locality in ministry, or the Local Non-Stipendiary Minister in the settlement itself. Whoever presides at the ministry of the Word and stands at the altar should not be there by chance or for a purely occasional and fleeting liturgical role. Apart from being part of the leadership of that local church in some way or other, they should be one who is able to carry the values, the hopes and fears of that community. The president of the Eucharist in the local church is one who from the soles of the feet to the top of the head knows what mission and ministry is happening here and how this particular community is related to the neighbourhood and to the wider Church through the diocese.

It has been the custom for such a person to be called by the community, by the bishop and by God, to be suitably educated, to have prayers said over them and hands laid upon them in public. To resist lay presidency is about an Anglican theology of Church. In an ecclesiology rooted in the Trinity there are no first and second class priests and no priests called to an entirely liturgical function. What is needed in the future – in the context of exciting new lay developments – are local non-stipendiary priests to ensure that such Eucharists as the local churches require are rooted in mission, unhurried, without the stress of ad-hoc arrangement, not dependent on retired clergy, however well-intentioned, and therefore undercutting every temptation to collude at clerical imperialism. It is said that the concept of community is a soft one – not easily defined, all to easily judged. What is meant by belonging to a Christian community will vary at different times and places. Those who preside at the Eucharist should normally be recognized as 'belonging' in some acceptable way to the locality in question. Just because the priest leader of the local church is present in a given church is no reason for him or her to *assume* the presidency at the eucharist normally taken by the NSM or LNSM.

For some dioceses the training of LNSMs is a central thrust in the development of Local Ministry. In others the development of local ministry is seen determinedly in terms of developing lay ministries and there can be fierce opposition to apparently encouraging clericalism. Both these viewpoints were reflected in the Edward King Institute 1994 Consultation. It was suggested there that to avoid the possibility of the development of LNSMs undermining lay ministry, any scheme needs to be set up in such a way as to emphasize the importance of all lay ministry as a gift from God, and only to select LNSMs from existing ministry teams through a process by which they are called out by the congregation.

The 1994 Consultation did not attempt to resolve this issue, but highlighted it as one that requires attention and further exploration. My own view is that to starve the churches of the priests required would in the end be seen to promote the clericalism that thrives on rarity value. To be a priest can be a wonderful ministry, but at the present time its serving character needs to be emphasized. We have seen that true priesthood cannot be recognized in isolation from community and that the future therefore should allow for a rich variety of ordained ministry so that the mission of the local church is not impeded or distorted.

Local Ministry is a Primary Agent of the Mission of the World Church

In the Church of England there is the double fear that what is local – in parishes and benefices – is either uncommitted to the diocese and Anglican Communion or else in danger of over-control by bishops and synods. As we have already explored, the very word 'local' when attached to 'ministry' raises lots of anxieties about yet another tier of maverick or unsupported church activity. However, we have also seen that there is a strong element in the Christian tradition that emphasizes that the local church is not a subsidiary branch of the universal, but is in fact as much of the world Church as it is possible to see in one place. Each local church in unique ways incarnates the catholic, universal Church which is a community of communities. The thrust of the ecumenical international debate about Church represented in the documents of Vatican II and of Lima, together with the seminal writings of Schillebeeckx and of Zizioulas, make this point at a deep level.

In the process of developing Local Ministry it will be vital to work for a strong mutual interplay in the relationship between the local and the wider Church for which different denominations each have their own structures and lines of communication. As increasingly Local Ministry Teams take on an ecumenical character it will be vital, if trust is to be maintained, for changes to be reflected in the relationships between regional church leaders and their education and training resource staff.

The nature of the relationship between the local, the regional and the world-wide must be part of the continuing debate about Local Ministry. The annual Bishop and Executive Leadership Institute – an educational event for about 40 participants sponsored by the Alban Institute in the USA – has provided a springboard for this essential part of the consideration of the future of the Church's ministry (Mead 1994). A brief reference to their main conclusions will provide a fitting ending to this book which aims to offer both encouragement to those engaged in the development of Local Ministry as well as to indicate the areas in which continuing research and debate are essential.

Elements to be Considered in the Relationship between the Local and the Wider Church

1. Where a small conflict escalates into a major dispute about liturgy, church reordering, keeping denominational rules, or the behaviour of a member of the Ministry Team, local churches need someone from the diocese or regional system to help get to the root of the trouble and formulate a strategy for dealing with it. Often these situations are undramatic and do not hit the press but the local church

needs someone from outside, with no investment except to provide a wider perspective on what is happening.

2. Usually the local church needs to be left to get on with the tasks it has set itself with its own energy. There is a danger that regional leaders – to keep themselves busy – overplay their role by, for example, pressing local churches to make declarations about strategy and new activity. The discernment lies in knowing which churches to leave alone and which to stimulate.

3. Part of the confident role of the bishop's officer or regional leader is to confront the local church when its policies seem to be in danger of cutting off that church from the mission of God or when practice is manifestly misguided or mismanaged. Here the judgement is to know who will be heard by the local church with a minimum of defensiveness. There are also issues about deciding on the legitimate freedom of the local church in the direction of its mission.

4. Even the most confident and effective church needs pastoral care on a regular basis. This keeping in touch makes it possible for it to be cared for in a crisis, such as breakdown of leadership or an unresolved battle in the church council.

5. Clergy in particular are under enormous stress today – financially, professionally and socially. Their role has taken a 180 degree turn in very recent times. We rely on them to lead the churches safely through the present transitional period of ministerial practice. Many were selected and trained with a very different role in view. The last thing they need is to be treated as problems or victims – this just exacerbates the situation. Part of a good pastoral role will be to insist that clergy engage in continuing programmes of learning. A sensitive, continuing relationship between the parish priest or local minister and the diocese or wider Church should make it possible for a sudden problem to be spotted and worked with before it gets out of control.

6. As we have seen throughout this book, changes in the way

the local church functions need consultancy and support from the diocese or wider Church – in terms of theological vision, strategies, training, and review. Some small churches in particular will be very dependent in a period of redevelopment on the encouragement and resources available to learn about leadership, effectiveness and communication skills. There is every reason why regional officers should act as brokers, enabling larger confident churches to share their resources with smaller ones.

7. Information and assistance about learning, financial problems, relating to other institutions at very basic levels may often be more necessary than might at first appear. This is another role for the regional leadership.

8. To be made to see the wider picture is a necessity at times for local churches. The bishop and regional education team have a special responsibility to help the local church have as wide a horizon as is possible and so to see themselves in the context of the mission of the whole Church. Part of this relationship will involve defusing recurring mistrust that local money is being squandered on bureaucracy or at least draining away vital local resources.

9. The local church needs to be sure someone is listening readily, regularly and accurately both when things are not going well and when they have something to celebrate. The idea of 'persistent friendship' between the local church and regional ministers suggests a model of overseeing which does not remain remote until there is trouble to be tackled but takes everything about the local with seriousness and joy, expecting and encouraging ever deeper patterns of maturity and discipleship.

EPILOGUE

This book is not presenting a single vision to the exclusion of all other futures for the Church of England. Traditional staffing of parishes with stipendiary clergy will obviously continue in some places as far into the future as it is possible to see now. Minster models or ecumenical clergy teams may emerge again in some parts.

What this book is about is facing up to the fact that the present uncertainty is not just a blip in the natural order of things so the future could be a comfortable return to the past. Even if more stipendiary clergy become available and even if, miraculously, church members opt to meet the necessary financial commitment, there is no turning back.

The complex context of society, Church, theology and organizational theory we have examined points to a strategy for local churches to exercise mission through the agency of ministry teams – a kaleidoscope of outcomes in different situations. Serving the triune God's mission for the completion of creation will always require fresh enquiries concerning the shape of the local church in itself and for others. Building on New Testament insights rooted in *communion* and developed as a trinitarian ecclesiology, churches are now to become models for and challenge structures that oppose the creation of redeemed relatedness in the practice of community life.

As I have identified, we shall travel far resourced by the rediscovery of a social trinitarian theology, consideration of the insights of philosophers and social theorists into power, awareness of the interpersonal processes of psychology, and a deliberate suspicion of all that closes churches off rather than lets them be available as an instrument for reordering the world and its people.

It is the proclamation and anticipation of God's Kingdom that is our aim, not maintaining any one form of Church – yet for the present moment God gives us the vehicle of the Church. As Paul challenges us not to be ashamed of the gospel, so we need to persevere to discover ways of being Church of which we can be proud. Nothing is sacred except our calling, which will involve a permanent disposition to letting go, discarding what has outlived its usefulness, never being afraid to let anything die.

In the end, however, confidence for the future of the churches lies only in not-knowing and powerlessness. We know we are called to maturity and to recognize our shining beauty as human beings called into God's future – in spite of our being damaged, having sinned, and regression into self-centredness. This Good News about God's promises made available to us by the Word made flesh through the Spirit is our chief resource. Standing vulnerable before the Trinity each day, recognizing our need to invite God to fill us with love and to transform us into pillars of fire is the key to the practice of authentic Christian community. As the Last Supper has inspired churches to wild improvisations of celebration – in art, liturgy and spirituality – so let Jesus' redeemed way of being with us and with the Father and the Spirit inspire us to the abundant practice of community that would otherwise be consistently impossible for us.

BIBLIOGRAPHY

Advisory Board of Ministry, *A Review of LNSM Schemes: Developments of Models of Ministry and Training in Recent Diocesan Proposals for LNSM*, ABM Ministry Paper No. 4, London, ABM Publications, 1992.

Archbishop of Canterbury's Commission on Urban Priority Areas, *Faith in the City: A Call for Action by Church and Nation*, London, Church House Publishing, 1985.

Archbishops' Commission on Rural Areas, *Faith in the Countryside*. Worthing, Churchman Publishing, 1990.

Avis, Paul, *Christians in Communion*. London, Chapman/Mowbray, 1990.

Barnett, James Monroe, *The Diaconate: A Full and Equal Order* (revised edition). Valley Forge, Trinity Press International, 1995.

Board of Mission, *A Time for Studying Ministry in Mission*, Occasional Paper No. 6. London, Church House Publishing, 1995.

Boff, C., in *Concilium 144: Tensions between the Churches of the First World and the Third World,* ed. Virgil Elizondo and Norbert Greinacher. Edinburgh, T. & T. Clark, 1981.

Boff, Leonardo, *Ecclesiogenesis: Base Communities Reinvent the Church*. London, Collins, 1986.

Boff, Leonardo, *Trinity and Society*. London, Burns & Oates, 1988.

Bonhoeffer, Dietrich, *Life Together*. London, SCM, 1949, reprinted 1992.

Bonhoeffer, Dietrich, 'Letters to a Friend', in *Letters and Papers from Prison*. London, Fontana, 1959.

Bosch, David, *Transforming Mission: Paradigm Shifts in the Theology of Mission*. New York, Orbis, 1994.

British Council of Churches, *The Forgotten Trinity*. London, British Council of Churches, 1991.

Bryne, James M., ed., *The Christian Understanding of God Today*. Dublin, The Columba Press, 1993.

Byrne, Lavinia, 'On Making Christian Community' (*Christian Community*, Winter 1993, No. 66, pp. 7f.).

Carey, George, and Hind, John, 'Ministry, Ministries, and the Ministry', in *Stepping Stones: Joint Essays on Anglican Catholic and Evangelical Unity,* ed. Christina Baxter, John Scott, and Roger Greenacre. London, Hodder & Stoughton, 1978.

Coriden, James, in George Dyer, *A Pastoral Guide to Canon Law.* Dublin, Gill & Macmillan, 1977.

Covey, Stephen R., *Principle Centred Leadership.* London, Simon & Schuster, 1992.

Davies, J. G., *New Perspectives on Worship Today.* London, SCM, 1978.

Dawn, Marva J., *The Hilarity of Community: Romans 12 and How to be the Church.* Leominster, Gracewing/Fowler Wright, 1993.

Day, T., *Dietrich Bonhoeffer on Christian Community and Common Sense,* New York, 1982.

Donovan, Vincent, *Christianity Rediscovered: An Epistle from the Masai.* London, SCM, 1982.

Dussel, Enrique, 'The Expansion of Christendom, Its crisis and the Present Moment' in *Concilium 144: Tensions between the Churches of the First World and the Third World.* Edinburgh, T. & T. Clark, 1981, pp. 44ff.

Dussel, Enrique, *Ethics and Community.* Maryknoll, Orbis, 1988.

Ecclestone, Alan (*Church Times,* 19 June 1992).

Farrell, E. J., *Disciples and other Strangers.* New Jersey, Dimension, 1974.

Fischer, Kathleen, *Women at the Well: Feminist Perspectives on Spiritual Direction,* London, SPCK, 1989.

Ford, David, *What happens in the Eucharist?* Society for the Study of Theology paper. Durham, 1995.

Foucault, M., *Discipline and Punish: The Birth of the Prison.* Harmondsworth, Penguin, 1977.

Fraser, Gillian SSC (*Christian Community,* 1993, No 66, p. 9).

Gill, Robin, *A Vision for Growth: Why your Church doesn't have to be a Pelican in the Wilderness.* London, SPCK, 1994.

Girard, René, *The Scapegoat.* Baltimore, Athlone Press, 1986.

Girard, René, with Jean-Michel Ourghoulian and Guy Lefort,

Things Hidden Since the Foundation of the World. London, Athlone Press, 1987.

Girard, René, *Job, the Victim of His People*. London, Athlone Press, 1987.

Gittins, Anthony J., 'The Mission of Transformation' *(Thinking Mission,* USPG, Issue 23, July 1995).

Greenwood, Robin, *Transforming Priesthood*. London, SPCK, 1994.

Greenwood, Robin, 'What Priesthood Now' *(Theology,* September/October 1995).

Gunton, Colin, *The Promise of Trinitarian Theology*. Edinburgh, T. & T. Clark, 1991.

Hauerwas, Stanley, *A Community of Character*. Notre Dame, University of Notre Dame Press, 1981.

Hauerwas, Stanley, *The Peacable Kingdom*. Notre Dame, University of Notre Dame Press, 1983.

Hauerwas, Stanley, *Christian Existence Today: Essays on Church, World, and Living in Between*. Durham, 1988.

Hill, William, *The Three Personed God: The Trinity as a Mystery of Salvation*. Washington DC, Catholic University of America Press, 1982.

Hiscox, Rhoda, *Celebrating Reader Ministry: 125 Years of Lay Ministry in the Church of England*. London, Mowbray, 1991.

Kelly, Anthony, *The Trinity of Love: A Theology of the Christian God*, New Theology Series. Wilmington, Delaware, Michael Glazier, 1989.

Kerkhofs, J., in L. Grollenberg, ed., *Minister? Pastor? Prophet? Grass Roots Leadership in the Churches*. London, SCM, 1980.

Kerkhofs, Jan, ed., *Europe Without Priests?* London, SCM, 1995.

King, Peter, *Dark Night Spirituality: Contemplation and the New Paradigm*. London, SPCK, 1995.

LaCugna, Catherine Mowry, *God for Us: The Trinity and Christian Life*. San Francisco, HarperCollins San Francisco, 1991.

Lehmann, Paul, *Ethics in a Christian Context*. New York, 1963.

Lovell, George, *Analysis and Design. A Handbook for Practitioners and Consultants in Church and Community Work*. London, Burns & Oates, 1995.

Lowe, Phil, and Lewis, Ralph, *Management Development Beyond the Fringe. A Practical Guide to Alternative Approaches.* New Jersey, Kogan Page, 1994.

Maggay, Melba, *Transforming Society.* Oxford, Lynx, 1994.

Martineau, Jeremy, *Turning the Sod...,* London, ACORA Publications, 1995.

McFadyen, Alastair I., *The Call to Personhood: A Christian Theory of the Individual in Social Relationships.* Cambridge, Cambridge University Press, 1991.

McGrath, Alister, *Understanding the Trinity,* Eastbourne, Kingsway, 1987.

Mead, Loren B., *Transforming Congregations for the Future,* One and Future Church Series Vol. 3. Bethesda, USA, Alban Institute, 1994.

Metz, J. B., *The Emergent Church: The Future of Christianity in a Post Bourgeois World.* London, SCM, 1981.

Milbank, John, *Theology and Social Theory.* Oxford, Blackwell, 1990.

Miller, Eric, *From Dependency to Autonomy: Studies in Organisation and Change.* London, Free Association Books, 1993.

Mitchell, B., *Mission and Ministry History and Theology in the Sacrament of Order,* Message of the Sacraments 6. Wilmington, Delaware, Michael Glazier, 1982.

Moltmann, Jürgen, *The Church in the Power of the Spirit.* London, SCM, 1975.

Moltmann, Jürgen, *Creating a Just Future.* London, SCM, 1989.

Moltmann, Jürgen, *The Trinity and the Kingdom of God: The Doctrine of God.* London, SCM, 1981.

Morgan, Gareth, *Images of Organization.* London, SAGE Publications, 1986.

Mouw, Richard J., *Consulting the Faithful: What Christian Intellectuals can Learn from Popular Religion.* Grand Rapids, Michigan, Eerdmans, 1994.

Obholzer, Anton, and Roberts, Vega Zagier, *The Unconscious at Work: Individuals and Organizational Stress in the Human Services.* London, Routledge, 1994.

Peters, Ted, *God as Trinity: Relationality and Temporality in Divine Life.* Louisville, Kentucky, Westminster/John Knox Press, 1993.

Polkinghorne, John, *Science and Christian Belief: Theological Reflections of a Bottom-up Thinker*. London, SPCK, 1994.

Rowland, Chris, and Vincent, John, eds., *Liberation Theology UK, British Liberation Theology 1*. Sheffield, Urban Theology Unit, 1995.

Schillebeeckx, E. *The Church with a Human Face: A New and Expanded Theology of Ministry*. London, SCM, 1985.

Schillebeeckx, E. *Church: The Human Story of God*. London, SCM, 1990.

Shüssler Fiorenza, E., *Bread not Stone: The Challenge of Feminist Biblical Interpretation*. Boston, 1984

Schwöbel, Christoph, and Gunton, Colin E., eds., *Persons, Human and Divine*. Edinburgh, T. & T. Clark, 1991.

Senge, Peter M., *The Fifth Discipline: The Art and Practice of the Learning Organisation*. London, Century Business, 1993.

Studer, Basil, *Trinity and Incarnation: The Faith of the Early Church*. Edinburgh, T. & T. Clark, 1993.

Suenens, Leon-Joseph, *Coresponsibility in the Church*. London, Burns & Oates, 1968.

Thiselton, Anthony C., *Interpreting God and the Postmodern Self: On Meaning, Manipulation and Promise*. Edinburgh, T. & T. Clark, 1995.

Thomas, R. S., *Collected Poems 1945–1990*, London, 1993.

Tiller, John, *A Strategy for the Church's Ministry*. London, Church Information Office for ACCM, 1983.

Torrance, T. F., *The Trinitarian Faith*. Edinburgh, T. & T. Clark, 1988.

Walters, J. Donald, *The Art of Supportive Leadership: A Practical Handbook for People in Positions of Responsibility*. Nevada City, California, Crystal Clarity, 4th edn, 1992.

Walton, Martin, *Marginal Communities: The Ethical Enterprise of the Followers of Jesus*. Kampen, The Netherlands, Kok Pharos, 1994.

Ward, Hannah, and Wild, Jennifer, *Guarding the Chaos: Finding Meaning in Change*. London, Darton, Longman & Todd, 1995.

Warren, Robert, *Building Missionary Congregations*, Board of Mission Occasional Paper No. 4. London, Church House Publishing, 1995.

Wilson, George B., *Wise Consultation by Leaders*. AVEC Consultation and Training Occasional Paper 6. London, AVEC, 1993.

World Council of Churches, *Baptism, Eucharist and Ministry* [Lima Text]. Geneva, World Council of Churches, 1982.

Zizioulas, John, *Being as Communion: Studies in Personhood and the Church*. New York, St Vladimir's Seminary Press, 1985.

INDEX

Advisory Board of Ministry
  10–11, 13
apostolicity 54
apostolic ministry 39
appointing clergy 86–7, 102–3
Archbishop's Commission on
  Rural Areas 68
ARCIC I 29
ARCIC II 29–30, 31, 32
authority: and power 92–6; in
  the New Testament 90–1;
  shared 89–90
Avec 97
Avis, Paul 29

baptism 13, 31, 39, 50, 63
Barry, F. R. 3
Barth, Karl 38
Base Communities 40
Basil of Caesarea 46
blessing, ministry of 77–9
Boff, Clodovis 40
Boff, Leonardo 40–1, 44, 47,
  57
Bonhoeffer, Dietrich 36, 62–3
Bosch, David 34
Byrne, Lavinia 89

Cappadocian theologians 46–7
Carey, George 69
Carr, Wesley 3
catholicity 52–4
change in the Church 104–6

collaborative ministry 38–9,
  61–5, 89–90
Commissioning Services 16
communion 29–32: Church as
  sign 48
conflict 86–9
consultation: local residents 15
contextual nature of Local
  Ministry 24, 58
Continuing Ministerial
  Education 70
Coriden, James 64
cosmos, destiny of 48, 56
cultural inclusivity 27–9

Davies, J. G. 34
diocese: and local church 103–
  4; role of 16–17, 23, 27, 102
discernment, role of priests
  71–7
Donovan, Vincent 58, 92
Dussel, Enrique 37–8

ecclesiology 25–43
Ecclestone, Alan 37
ecumenical insights 29–30, 33
Edward King Institute 1994
  Consultation 11, 23, 100–8:
  definition of Local Ministry
  5–6, 101; recommendations
  11
episcopate, ministry of 27
Eucharist 50: and community

30–1; lay presidency 106–8; priest's role 74–7

evangelism 54–6

Exploring Local Ministry 15

Faith in the City 14, 29, 35

Faith in the Countryside 14, 68

Farrell, E. 21

Ford, David 75

Foucault, Michel 92–3, 95–6

Fraser, Gillian 89

Gill, Robin 15

Girard, René 63

Gloucester Diocese 11, 12–21

Goethe, J. von 56

Green, Michael 3

Greenwood, Robin 45–6

Gregory of Nazianzus 46, 67

Gregory of Nyssa 46

Guildford Diocese 10

Gunton, Colin 47, 56

Hanson, A. T. 3

Hauerwas, Stanley 36–7, 38

Hereford Diocese 10

hierarchy 65–8

Hill, William 46

Hind, John 69

Hiscox, Rhoda 68

holiness of Church 52

House of Bishops 13, 33, 84

images of Church 44, 57–9

inclusiveness 34–6

Jenkins, David 62

John the Baptist 67, 85

Kenya, Province of 28

Kerkhofs, Jan 9, 39

King, Peter 100

koinonia 29–32, 37, 41, 48

Lambeth Quadrilateral 27

Lehmann, Paul 36

liberation theology 34–5

licensing 17, 102

Lichfield Diocese 10

Lima Documents 14, 38–9, 64, 109

Lincoln Diocese 13

Liverpool Diocese 10

local church 25–43: and wider Church 22–3, 26, 36, 108–11; as area of collaborative ministry 26–7

Local Ministry 9–24: and mission 108–11; benefits 17–21; Gloucester scheme 12–21; management 82–4; problems 81–2, 84–6

Local Ministry Officers 15, 16, 85–6

Local Ministry Teams 102–3

Local Non-Stipendiary Ministry 10, 13, 17

local neighbourhood 72–3

Lovell, George 98

Lumen Gentium 22, 65

management 82–4, 96–9

Mead, Loren 109
Metz, J. B. 41
Milbank, John 34
mission: and ministry 21–23, 63–4; of local church 33–4
Mitchell, B. 54
models of ministry teams 10–11, 12–13
Moltmann, Jürgen 41–2, 57
Mouw, Richard 51

New Testament: on communion 30; on authority 90–1
Nicaea, Council of 46
Non-Stipendiary Ministers 16, 107–8

Old Testament on communion 29–30

Parochial Church Councils 15, 16, 17, 23, 85
partnership of clergy and laity 13, 22, 23 *see also* collaborative ministry
peace, sharing the 34
Polkinghorne, John 59
Porvoo Document 64
power: and authority 92–6; in the New Testament 90–1; theories of 91–6
priests 66, 70–80: appointing 86–7, 102–3
Puebla Document 41, 64

Ramsey, Michael 3
Readers 16, 27, 68–70
Robinson, John 3
Roland, Allen 3
Roman Catholic Church 9, 64, 82
Rowland, Chris 38
rural communities 24, 26

Schillebeeckx, Edward 14, 100, 109
Schüssler Fiorenza, E. 42
Schwöbel, Christoph 42–3, 47
Senge, Peter 98
Southwark Diocese 10

Temple, William 55
Thomas, R. S. 75, 79
Thiselton, Anthony 53
Tillich, Paul 38
Tiller, John 3, 14, 28
trinitarian theology 31, 32, 43, 44–59: history 46–8
Trinity, image of priesthood 71
Truro Diocese 10

unity, mark of Church 49–51
urban communities 24, 26

Vincent, John 38

Walters, J. Donald 70
Walton, Martin 41

Ward, Hannah 81
Warren, Robert 13, 56, 58
Wesley and Methodist Studies
    Centre 97
Wild, Jennifer 81
Wilson, George 88–9

Winchester Diocese 10
witness of priests 79–80

Zizioulas, John 46, 57, 67,
    109